Praise for *Get the Life*

'I am deeply inspired by Phil Par
and practical. In Get the Life You Love, NOW he reveals
what you really need to 'dû' to experience a life you love.'
Robert Holden, author of *Loveability* and *Shift Happens!*

'Given that 90 per cent of doctor's visits are the result of
stress, stress-reducing techniques like the ones taught in
Phil Parker's book can be not only life-saving, but happiness-
saving. With power tools aimed at helping you unravel
limiting beliefs and self-sabotaging behaviours that keep you
from thriving, this book is just what the doctor ordered.'
**Lissa Rankin MD, *New York Times* bestselling
author of *Mind Over Medicine***

'To live a happy life requires different attitudes as well as new
skills. Phil Parker's amazing new book provides an enjoyable and
practical way to gain both. His great skill as a storyteller and his
easy writing style breathe life into the usually turgid NLP genre.'
**Robbie Steinhouse, author of *Think Like an Entrepreneur*,
Brilliant Decision Making and *How to Coach with NLP***

'Phil Parker is a miracle worker who really walks his talk. His
dedication to the wellness and happiness of others shines
through his work, and he is always willing to support the
healing and growth of all those he comes across. I have
the pleasure of calling Phil my friend and I am mesmerized
by the radical shifts his Lightning Process has created
for others. This book is filled with love and integrity.'
Kyle Gray, author of *Angel Prayers* and *The Angel Whisperer*

'An incredible collection of easy-to-get ideas that bring super-fast
results. Phil's life-healing strategies are based upon truth and
his lifetime of experience. There is excellence on each page!'
**Derek Mills, international speaker, mentor and
author of *The 10-Second Philosophy*®**

PHIL PARKER

GET
THE LIFE
YOU
LOVE
NOW

HOW TO USE THE LIGHTNING PROCESS®
TOOLKIT FOR HAPPINESS AND FULFILMENT

HAY HOUSE

Carlsbad, California • New York City • London • Sydney
Johannesburg • Vancouver • Hong Kong • New Delhi

First published and distributed in the United Kingdom by:
Hay House UK Ltd, Astley House, 33 Notting Hill Gate, London W11 3JQ
Tel: +44 (0)20 3675 2450; Fax: +44 (0)20 3675 2451
www.hayhouse.co.uk

Published and distributed in the United States of America by:
Hay House Inc., PO Box 5100, Carlsbad, CA 92018-5100
Tel: (1) 760 431 7695 or (800) 654 5126
Fax: (1) 760 431 6948 or (800) 650 5115
www.hayhouse.com

Published and distributed in Australia by:
Hay House Australia Ltd, 18/36 Ralph St, Alexandria NSW 2015
Tel: (61) 2 9669 4299; Fax: (61) 2 9669 4144
www.hayhouse.com.au

Published and distributed in the Republic of South Africa by:
Hay House SA (Pty) Ltd, PO Box 990, Witkoppen 2068
Tel/Fax: (27) 11 467 8904
www.hayhouse.co.za

Published and distributed in India by:
Hay House Publishers India, Muskaan Complex, Plot No.3, B-2,
Vasant Kunj, New Delhi 110 070
Tel: (91) 11 4176 1620; Fax: (91) 11 4176 1630
www.hayhouse.co.in

Distributed in Canada by:
Raincoast, 9050 Shaughnessy St, Vancouver BC V6P 6E5
Tel: (1) 604 323 7100; Fax: (1) 604 323 2600

Text © Phil Parker, 2013

A catalogue record for this book is available from the British Library.

ISBN: 978-1-78180-174-1

Printed and bound in Great Britain by TJ International, Padstow, Cornwall.

To the inspirational Natasha

Contents

Acknowledgements

I'd like to thank all of those who supported me through the decades of research that led to this book: especially my core team Lydia and Helen (both of whom worked all hours reviewing this book), Fiona, Claire, Lisa and Sarah, and past members Ros and Ellie. Thanks go to my kids, friends, family and the super six Hay House authors – Robert, David, Ali, Derek and John – for their generosity and time. And thanks also to my PhD supervisor, Dr Esther Murray, for her humour and support, and to Jill for her incredible contribution.

Thanks as ever goes to all those working hard behind the scenes in the Hay House family worldwide for helping to get this out to you, and to Sandy, my long-suffering editor.

INTRODUCTION

Start Here...

If you want a life you love, starting right NOW, then this book is for you.

It's designed to take you through the steps of my world-changing Lightning Process® (LP), which will dramatically improve your levels of happiness, your sense of fulfilment and your future.

WHAT YOU'LL LEARN

This immensely practical book will take you on quite a journey, which is divided into three phases:

Awakening

In which you may be surprised to discover that **you are a genius** after all. Don't worry if that doesn't quite sound like you, as I'm absolutely certain, no matter how far off being a genius you feel right now, that *is* going to change after reading this book.

You'll also learn to identify how and when you're getting in the way of your own happiness and fulfilment.

Integration

You'll be guided through the precise steps required to instantly change your mood and start to uncover solutions so you can **be empowered in any situation.**

Resilience

You'll learn tools based on the latest research into how the brain learns – to make these **changes actually stick…**

So you can start living the life you love NOW.

THIS BOOK IS FOR YOU IF…

You want to address the type of issues listed below:

- Unhappiness, sadness, hopelessness, feeling flat
- Low self-esteem, self-doubt, uncertainty, perfectionism, fear of failure
- Stress, feeling overwhelmed
- Cravings, smoking, overeating
- Struggle, boredom, lack of purpose, procrastination
- Guilt, feeling you are responsible for everyone else's problems or others' happiness
- Blaming others, feeling like a victim or bystander in your life
- Frustration, anger, repetitive thoughts

Or want even more…

- Vitality, enthusiasm, motivation, excitement, positivity, boost to your health
- Confidence, to be present, to feel more connected
- To improve your inner/self-talk
- Love, peace, happiness, fulfilled relationships
- To seize the moment, take responsibility for your life, be someone who makes things happen
- To like or love every aspect of yourself
- To know you can do it, and do the things you say you want to do
- To make the most of your life, be who you want to be, be the most powerful force in your life

LIFE'S TOO SHORT
NOT TO HAVE
A GREAT ONE
RIGHT NOW.

This final point reminds me of the brilliant passage by George Bernard Shaw:

'I rejoice in life for its own sake. Life is no "brief candle" to me. It is sort of a splendid torch which I have a hold of for the moment, and I want to make it burn as brightly as possible before handing it over to future generations.'

So, if you want some of this and you're prepared to work for it, this book will give you the chance to change your life.

WHAT ARE THE ORIGINS OF THE TEACHINGS IN THIS BOOK AND THE LP?

I designed the Lightning Process after researching and working in a number of areas.

First, I spent a long time considering the question, from both my personal and professional experience:

What makes for a happy life?

Second, I became skilled in the transformational fields of NLP (neuro-linguistic programming, an approach for making rapid change), coaching, osteopathy (a holistic physical therapy) and the mind–body connection.

Although you might be able to identify some elements of these methods in the LP, it's much more than simply a mixture of these approaches. Certainly that's the experience of the many NLP experts and osteopaths who use the LP to finally make the changes that have eluded them previously.

Third, there seems to be an element of fundamental human wisdom in the Lightning Process, as many of the thousands of people I've helped get the lives they love have told me how well the Lightning Process fits with the core teachings of many spiritual philosophies – approaches that, until that point, I hadn't studied. It also resonates with many of the core ideas behind newer philosophical approaches, such as Eckhart Tolle's *The Power of Now* (coincidentally published in the same year I designed the LP) and Rhonda Byrne's *The Secret*.

This suggests to me that there are some core skills or concepts we need to learn as humans to have great lives. Throughout history the great mystics and philosophers have stumbled upon them and attempted to make them available to all. Unfortunately all too often people found that it was pretty difficult to work out what these great minds were saying or to put those concepts into practice.

However, I think the following simple question deserves a simple and practical answer:

What do I need to do to get a great life?

Based on my experience, of what actually works in the real world, that's exactly what you are holding in your hands now.

And because life's too short not to have a great one right NOW, let's get to it...

PART I
Awakening

*'Remember not getting what you want is
sometimes a wonderful stroke of luck.'*

DALAI LAMA

The first part of the journey to getting a life you love explores
how, somehow, we often manage to avoid getting the life we
love; how the essential element to any change is recognizing
what we need to change and when to take action. And so Part I
is all about getting a fresh perspective on these important
areas – one that is eye-opening and life changing.

CHAPTER 1

Where It All Begins

My journey in designing the Lightning Process and writing this book, as with so many extraordinary adventures, started with a crisis.

I was 21, in my first year of osteopathic college and a professional guitarist, when I came across something devastating, which was to change my life forever…

SHARKS!

They're really dangerous with their rows of razor-sharp teeth! But it wasn't a shark that caused me such devastating problems. Strangely enough, it was something much more sinister. Yes, that killer machine…

THE FAMILY CARAVAN!

Or more precisely the glass within its back window.

We were all pushing the caravan as it had become stuck in a dip, so we began rocking it backwards and forwards to free it. I was leaning heavily with my outstretched palms flat against the rear window, as I done many times before, when my left hand cracked the window and plunged through the glass, lacerating my wrist. This was bad enough, but because the others continued to rock the caravan, unaware of the developing situation, the broken glass also rocked backwards and forwards on my outstretched arm and wrist.

From my detailed knowledge of the anatomy of the forearm, which I'd just covered in the previous academic year at college, I knew this was not a good thing.

Narrowly missing slicing the main arteries, which would have caused my very rapid death, instead I had severed a number of muscles and one of the major nerves of my hand. This nerve, the ulnar nerve, is also called the musician's nerve as it supplies the signals to the muscles needed to perform the delicate movements required by a musician in order to play an instrument.

DOCTORS AND A GYPSY JAZZ GUITARIST

When I discovered the extent of my injuries at the hospital, I knew it was very bad news. Once a nerve is severed it can no longer transmit signals from the brain to the muscles and, just like pulling the power cable out of computer, the muscles just don't work any more. Furthermore, to get things back to normal, the nerve has to regrow from where it was cut and find its way to the particular set of muscle fibres it is supposed to be controlling.

The surgeon told me that a complete recovery was extremely unlikely. He told me that 'neurologically speaking' I was 'old' and, even if my nervous system did, by some remote chance, get a burst of youthfulness and regrow, the chances of it growing in the right direction and reconnecting with all the muscles were minimal to impossible.

His prognosis: 'You'll never be able to move your fingers again.'

This was the worst possible news. After all, there aren't that many one-handed osteopaths or guitarists! My dreams and career were over, my future destroyed. But this new future was not the one I wanted, so I immediately sought a second opinion.

The second surgeon said, 'You will never be able to move your fingers again; you will be left with a claw hand.'

Not the answer I wanted either. I wanted to recover my hand function and my future depended on it. Sure, I could get by in life with just one functioning hand, but not in the careers I'd set my sights on. I kept thinking: *Surely there **must** be a way*.

To be honest, much to my parents' and teachers' annoyance, I've always been a bit like this. If someone says you can't do something, a part of me always wonders and questions whether

4

that's actually true. So, I followed the doctor's rehab advice while seeking additional medical and alternative therapy opinions. But I just kept being given the same message: 'You're out of luck, your hand will never recover.'

In spite of this, I kept asking different people and eventually found Romy Paine, an inspiring physiotherapist, who agreed with me that there was no reason why I couldn't make a full recovery.

I also came across another important figure, and one who was to play a large role in the creation of the Lightning Process and this book, albeit years after his death. His name was Django Reinhardt and he was a Gypsy Jazz guitarist. He played the guitar brilliantly until he was caught in a fire that raged, by bizarre coincidence, through his caravan. His left hand was burned so badly that he could barely use two of his fingers, and had to completely relearn to play the guitar. Yet, despite his injuries, Django went on to create a whole new musical style and is considered to be one of the most significant guitarists of the 1930s.

In case you're wondering, I did recover. After just three months, I began to see signs of improvement and was playing the guitar within six months. But what's more, I did work as an osteopath and I did become a professional guitarist, record albums and play to huge crowds. But I wondered why I got better, in spite of the hugely negative, but well-informed, medical opinions. What enabled me to be able to use my hand again, when I saw so many other people with the same injury, both when I was in rehab and later as a clinician, who just didn't? When I looked back at this time, I was struck by a number of things. First, I'm certain that the medical care helped, but I think of even more significance were:

- My determination to recover.

- The importance of fully recovering – coping with one hand meant giving up my future plans.

- My decision to keep on asking for opinions, hoping to find someone who would support the possibility of my recovery, despite all the negative medical assessments.

- Finding someone medically qualified who believed I could recover.
- Choosing to ignore the balance of opinion (I only ever found one other person who agreed that I could recover).
- Finding someone else who had been through something very similar to me and overcome impossible odds.

I'm also indebted to that younger me who led me doggedly from disaster, through hopelessness to success. That journey definitely changed my life path and confirmed my view that we really need to understand and harness the power of the mind to influence our body, our life and our future.

It also made me realize that, even when the world really seems to be against us, and everything looks like it's going wrong, it's just a phase, just part of the journey, and we will look back at some point and see it for what it really is – some kind of opportunity. The Dalai Lama best summed up this perspective when he said, 'Remember that not getting what you want is sometimes a wonderful stroke of luck.'

EVEN WHEN **THE WORLD** REALLY SEEMS TO BE **AGAINST US,** AND EVERYTHING LOOKS LIKE IT'S **GOING WRONG,** IT'S **JUST A PHASE,** JUST **PART OF THE JOURNEY.**

CHAPTER 2

Prepare for Take-off

Working through this book will be a bit like hanging out with me for a few days, so it's probably useful to get a sense of my approach to the process of change. I believe:

- that change happens best when undertaken with kindness, compassion and fun. And if it's not fun, it's probably not worth doing.

- that everything should be able to be simply explained; being so clever you can write books that very few understand only means you can't explain it very well.

- there are many things that we think of as being 'impossible', but often that's only because we haven't done them yet.

- that change takes very little time.

- we need to be bold and embrace new, unexpected ways of looking at things; a must for this 'road trip for the mind and soul' of a book.

If you're reading this book about change then you're likely to share some of these ideas, so welcome aboard. But, before we set off, let's run at full speed through some ground rules to make the journey ahead easier. Once you've got your head around those then we can start to crack on with the main job, which is to have a brilliant life NOW.

WHO ARE YOU GOING TO BE?

I would love to be there with you as you read this book, helping you work out what was going on, what was keeping you stuck, to coach, assist and support you. But, obviously, I'm not. So naturally this role is going to fall to you, as no one else will be checking to make sure you're doing what's needed.

Many people have commented that getting what you want requires a commitment to doing whatever it takes. In that spirit, this first exercise is designed to help you actually get something from this book, rather than it just being another self-help book providing interesting ideas with no real change.

Also, at this point, it might be helpful to start a journal or workbook, so that you can write down your answers as you work through the exercises and elements of this book, as well as any notes that seem relevant.

Exercise: the elements of success

Take a moment to think about a personal success story, or one experienced by someone you know. Write down your answers.

- What were the three core elements that made that success happen?
- What three things are you going to do to make sure that you apply these incredible tools so you can get what you want out of life?
- Finally, knowing yourself better than anybody else does, what are your key ways of getting in the way of success? There are a 1,001 possibilities but sabotaging strategies might include, for example, suddenly finding the idea of cleaning out that cupboard much more captivating than reading this book or doing the exercises; reminding yourself how nothing ever really works, so it's not worth bothering; or channelling your energy and time into putting other people first and neglecting your needs because you feel you don't deserve it at some level. Make a list now of your top five sabotaging strategies.

- By the way, it's fine to have sabotaging strategies, everyone does, just don't go off track by beating yourself up for having them. Instead, just congratulate yourself for recognizing their presence. Becoming aware of the kinds of things that have kept you stuck is the first step to change. Once you've recognized them, you can then use the tools in the following chapters to deal with them, so they'll no longer have any power over you.

- Finally, just for a moment, consider what would that be like – to have finally resolved this stuff, once and for all?

INFLUENCE

The previous exercise echoes one of the themes running through most of my work – the idea of 'influence'. For clarity, let's begin with a definition. Being someone with an influence means:

- Having a say in how things turn out.

- Being able to make a difference to what happens next.

Central to this is recognizing:

A. Which things you do have the power to make a difference to – the things you can influence;

B. Which you don't – the things you can't influence.

Using your 'influence' is to take action to make a difference to those things that fit into group A.

Later we'll discuss how to recognize which parts of a situation we can influence and which parts we can't, and also how to deal with those times when there seems to be nothing we can change. You may be surprised to discover that, actually, you are more influential in your life than you ever could imagine.

This self-empowering idea of influence allows us to recognize and utilize the power we have to change our lives for the better. For most people, this sense of empowerment is freeing and life-enhancing. For others, however, this idea of having a say in what

THERE ARE **TWO KINDS OF PEOPLE**: THOSE WHO **THINK THEY CAN** AND THOSE WHO **THINK THEY CAN'T,** AND THEY'RE **BOTH RIGHT.**

happens next can, initially at least, appear to have some unwanted consequences. In this case, the idea of influence may:

- Result in a person feeling overwhelmed by the thought of taking responsibility for making a difference;

- Create a feeling of disquiet due to the realization that if they want change then they're going to have to take action personally, rather than relying on others to make the change happen for them.

On closer examination, however, most people begin to see that these consequences are actually good news.

First, realizing that feeling overwhelmed when it's time to make changes highlights one of the key issues this book will help you to resolve.

Second, knowing you are the one who's in charge of making that change empowers you to recognize that you have a free hand in redesigning your future.

Third, although other people can help you, you start to realize that you don't actually *need* anybody else to make it happen. So you are free to start to create the future you want because you have the essential people needed to make it happen – and that's just you – already here.

The final potential consequence of 'rediscovering your influence' is that some people misunderstand it as feeling as if they are to blame or, as it's sometimes phrased, 'responsible' for the problem. You can see how they figure this out – it's a mistake, but quite a reasonable flow of ideas, and goes something like this:

- If they now realize they have the potential to influence a problem they have been stuck with;

- They now see they have the possibility of changing it;

- They can then create a sense that they 'should' have changed this before now.

However, this is a complete distraction. When we look at the idea of influence it's really not relevant why it has not changed before;

the only thing that's important is what happens next. We'll cover this aspect in more depth in the chapter on 'beliefs' (*see page 219*).

Influence and blame are like two polar opposites; when people feel blame it usually disempowers them, so they become less and less influential. When people are truly being influential in their future in a positive way, there is an absence of blame because the focus is entirely on the question:

How do we make things different?

Try out this idea of influence and learn to distinguish it from blame by using the exercise that follows.

Exercise: The bus driver

Imagine you're a passenger on a bus being driven by a person with diabetes who has failed to look after their blood sugar levels for the last few days. The driver slumps into a coma at the wheel and the bus heads towards the oncoming traffic…

'Who is "to blame" or "responsible" for the impending disaster?'

I would imagine your answer would be along the following lines: clearly it's the bus driver; their job is to be fit for work and well enough to drive the passengers around safely.

However, if we ask the influence question:

'Who can influence what happens next?'

Your answer is likely to be: 'anyone who can get to the steering wheel in time'.

Therefore, you have effectively distinguished 'blame' from 'influence'.

STORIES

Throughout this book I'll be using stories as one of the ways to explain things. At first glance, this might seem like an unfamiliar way of helping change occur but, actually, it's a very powerful way of starting to shift things that might have been stuck for a long time. One of the reasons for this is that most people try to use logic and rationale to work their way out of a particular stuck way of thinking but when that doesn't work are unsure what to do next – except to try, once again, to work through the issue, logically and rationally.

It seems this is a common default setting for dealing with problems for which we can't find solutions. If our plan doesn't work and we have no other options, we just try the same solutions again and again. Unfortunately, this just makes us feel that there is no solution rather than leading us to a realization that we are using an approach that we've already demonstrated isn't going to work.

For example, you're about to leave the house, but discover you've lost your keys. You look in the three places you know they must be: the table, your other clothes' pockets and your bag. But when you don't find them, you check the table, your pockets and bag again...

However, stories don't use that rational, logical part of the brain, which has failed to come up with a solution so far; they access very different parts of the brain, which involves thinking in more creative and unconscious ways. In fact, recent research[1] shows that this type of non-linear thinking is a very important part of coming up with new solutions. In one study, a group of students were asked to come up with new uses for a familiar object. Then they were asked to stop the task and split into three groups. The first group was asked to have a break, the second group was asked to focus very hard on a new subject, and the third group was asked to engage in an activity that encouraged their minds to wander. All three groups were then asked to perform the original task again. This time, the members of the third group, the daydreamers, were able to come up with 41 per cent more possibilities than either of the other two groups.

So, you can see how stories can be a helpful mechanism in understanding things from a new point of view, processing things at a different level and useful in explaining some of the more complicated concepts in simple ways.

This next section on beliefs starts with some stories.

BELIEFS ARE YOUR PASSPORT TO SUCCESS

When travelling through foreign lands you need to ensure that you have the correct visas, passports and other documentation prepared before starting off. Your beliefs will be your passport to success on this journey, so before going any further you'll need to check your papers are in order…

Jumping fleas

A man who owned a travelling flea circus once shared with me the secret of his success. For those of you who don't know, a travelling flea circus is a tiny circus in which all the acrobatics are performed by jumping fleas, instead of humans.

Confidentially he informed me that the real trick of having a successful travelling flea circus is to have the best jumping fleas. And the best jumping fleas are found in the high Mexican desert. The problem with these Mexican jumping fleas is that they jump incredibly high, as high as a horse and, as a result, are very difficult to catch and even more difficult to train.

'The secret,' he said, 'is to know about how much these Mexican jumping fleas love to have fiestas. For not many people know that every full moon is a cause for celebration for these fleas, and the way they like to celebrate involves drinking strong tequila and dancing wildly through the night to mariachi bands.'

So whenever he was passing that way he waited for the moon to be full. He would sneak into the desert, listening intently for the tiny giveaway sounds of wild whooping, the shaking of maracas and the scent of tequila.

Then the next morning, while the Mexican jumping fleas slept off their dreadful hangovers in the long cool shade of a cactus, he would place a jam jar carefully over each one. He carried a suitcase with a selection of crystal-clear glass jam jars of different sizes for exactly this moment.

As the morning rolled on, the fleas would wake with tequila-sized headaches and, as they always did, jump as high as a horse into the air. But unexpectedly, just a few inches after take-off, their already sore heads came into contact with the bottom of the upturned glass jar. Shocked, they tumbled to the ground and in an attempt to escape, jumped again. They rose off the ground only to find that once again they hit something, tumbled down dazed, confused and hurting, but desperate to escape jumped again and again.

Now, not surprisingly, it doesn't take long for a hungover Mexican jumping flea to realize something is wrong and accommodate this new, unexpected experience.

'Within minutes,' he told me, 'you can observe the Mexican jumping fleas jumping, but now instead of jumping as high as they can, they adapt so they jump to just below the glass ceiling of the jam jar.'

After just a few hours, he carefully removed the glass jars, but as the fleas were now only jumping to just below where the jar was, they never found out that there was nothing stopping them jumping to their full potential. And as the jam jars were different heights, he had effectively trained them to jump to the heights that he specifically wanted.

He finished his tale with a sigh, 'It's sad,' he confided, 'to notice what happens when fleas from other circuses retire from their long service in circus work. For even though they are still capable of it, they never jump to their full ability ever again, continuing to jump precisely to the height of their original jam-jar prison.'

I, however, owe my fleas a debt of gratitude for their work and make it my mission to retrain my retired fleas back to their normal exuberant jumping height. It makes my heart glad to watch them leaping away, in search of the next full-moon fiesta...'

Four-minute mile

Until 6 May 1954, it was considered a fundamental truth that humans couldn't run a mile in any less than four minutes. Many people had tried to break this barrier, but it just seemed to be a physical impossibility; after all the human body, like any other complex machine, must have limits, and this seemed to be one of them.

And then on that Thursday in Oxford, Roger Bannister broke that barrier, running a mile in three minutes and 59 seconds.

What happened next was even more fascinating, as many other athletes who'd tried and failed to breach the four-minute barrier in the previous months and years also found they could now break that limit. They hadn't become any better trained or even faster, they just now knew, or believed, it was possible.

Both these stories illustrate how beliefs often get in the way of having a life you love, or as Henry Ford so eloquently said: 'There are two kinds of people: those who think they can, and those who think they can't, and they're both right.'

Your beliefs are incredibly important, so start by using the following exercises to get yours working for you.

Exercise: Possible or impossible?

Having read the stories on pages 16–18, check your beliefs are aligned with what you want to achieve and answer this important question:

It is possible or impossible for me to get a life I love?

Hopefully you realize now that, of course, it is possible.

Be inspired

Take a moment to use the following powerful process to help enhance your positive beliefs even further. Keep a record of your answers in your workbook.

- What belief about change would you love to have?
- Who do you know who would fully support and champion that belief for you?
- Imagine if they were with you now, what would they say to you?
- If they were to give you a gift that symbolized their message to you, what would it be?
- Accept that gift and choose to place it somewhere within you that feels right.
- Notice how it feels to move on through the book with their presence always with you.

CHAPTER 3

Lesson 1: Genius 101

Let's start with a topic that many people dealing with unhappiness and lack of fulfilment may find a little bit surprising: genius and the study of excellence.

I've been fascinated by the idea of genius and excellence for decades and have spent a lot of time working with and talking to people at the top of their fields. My role was to research what made these high-achieving athletes, explorers, musicians, actors and entrepreneurs so good at what they did, and to discover if it was possible to learn how to replicate their success.

As a result, I learned a few things about genius and excellence that I'd like to share with you. First, my best way of describing genius is someone who is able to:

Consistently
Reproduce
Great results
On demand

This description of genius seems to apply fairly universally. When you think about it the best football players are able to deliver the ball with pinpoint accuracy time and time again just when it is needed; the best musicians are able to deliver a passionate flawless performance, night after night, and so on.

But there's another factor that needs to be added to the list. To understand it we need to look at idea of the 'four stages of learning', as understood and described by Noel Burch (1970) and William Howell.[2]

FOUR STAGES OF LEARNING

1. Unconscious incompetence

This is the first step of learning and occurs when we don't even recognize that we are not good at this skill; possibly we don't even value it or know it exists. Deciding to become good at this skill involves moving into the next phase.

2. Conscious incompetence

Here we recognize the deficit in our skill set and start to work to become proficient; we're just beginning, so we're not great at it yet. Further practice moves us to the next phase.

3. Conscious competence

This is where we are now mastering the skill but still have to be very consciously aware of exactly what we're doing while doing it and stay focused so that we perform effectively.

4. Unconscious competence

Once we become very proficient at something, and our geniuses are good examples of this, we reach this final level.

This is where we don't even need to think or concentrate on doing the task any more, we just do it automatically. Therefore, we can expand our definition to a genius is able to:

Consistently
Reproduce
Great results
On demand
Unconsciously and automatically

This is great news because the automatic functioning of the brain is very precise, rapid and reliable. You might notice this with things such as walking, breathing or signing your name. You have become very unconsciously competent at doing these things and can do them without having to concentrate at all.

And this brings us to one of the core themes of this book, how the brain changes as we learn, and the concept of neuroplasticity.

NEUROPLASTICITY

I'm going to cover this fascinating subject quite briefly here as I've already written about it in depth in many of my other books. Fortunately, in spite of its long name, it is actually quite easy to understand and vitally important for your future.

The most important thing to understand is that brain science used to be based on the theory that the brain was 'hardwired', like an electrical circuit board – so, once the pathways were laid down, they were believed to be there forever. However, recent advances in neuroscience have revealed a new understanding of the brain – it's now seen as being much more similar to a group of muscles. As you know, if you exercise one particular group of muscles a lot they become stronger, and if you forget to exercise another group of muscles they waste away.

It appears that the brain pathways work the same way. The more you use a pathway in your brain, the more easily it is triggered and the faster and stronger it becomes; equally, the less you use it, the more it fades away.

For example, have you noticed how a child's grades can change in the same subject depending on how much they get on with their teacher?

Imagine you have an unpleasant and boring teacher for science one term. When you think about science lessons, you create a signal that travels along a nerve until it reaches a gap, called a 'synapse', which it has to jump across (using chemical neurotransmitters) to allow the signal to be carried on to its final destination. At the gap, the signal has the chance to be carried by two or more different nerves, which go to different final destinations.

Let's imagine one is for happiness and the other boredom.

You don't like science lessons with this teacher, so the signal jumps to the boredom nerve and triggers the boredom pathway. As a result of using this pathway regularly, the brain starts to

THE **MORE** YOU **USE** ANY **PATHWAY** IN YOUR **BRAIN,** THE MORE **EASILY** IT IS **TRIGGERED** AND THE **FASTER** AND **STRONGER** IT BECOMES.

rearrange itself physically so those two nerves 'science' and 'boredom' actually move closer together, to make it even easier for the signal to travel along the pathway.

This is neuroplasticity, the ability of the brain to change as a result of use. It's like your brain saying 'Well, if you're going to use it a lot, I'll make it easier for you.'

The brain is very helpful like that! Interestingly, it doesn't really mind which pathways are being strengthened, it's just following the rule of, 'if you use it, I'll make it easier'.

Imagine that, luckily, the following year you have a brilliantly inspirational science teacher. Now when the 'science' pathway signal gets to the gap it heads towards the 'happiness' pathway. After a very short time, the new nerve friends of 'science' and 'happiness' move towards each other to make it easier for the signal to travel along this pathway, and the connection between the 'science' and 'boredom' pathways diminishes as they grow apart. Now it's not so easy to trigger the science–boredom pathway and much easier to trigger the science–happiness pathway.

You can see neuroplasticity at work in the following exercise.

Exercise: Who's in control of your brain?

Lift your right foot up off the floor and makes circles with it in a clockwise direction. Now with your hand draw a number six in the air.

Did you notice what your foot just did?

Most people find that their foot begins to move in an anticlockwise direction as soon as they draw the six.

At some point the brain learned that as we often use our feet and hands at the same time, it would be useful to connect up the feet and hand pathways, using neuroplasticity.

Powerful stuff, eh?

So neuroplasticity has great significance in the creation of habits, genius and change. And throughout this book you'll learn how you can use it to make changes to a whole interesting set of brain pathways.

THE DOWNSIDE OF UNCONSCIOUS COMPETENCE

As we've discovered from the last exercise, neuroplasticity is great at making us really good at things without us having to think about them – our 'unconscious competence', mentioned earlier (*see page 22*). The downside to this is that it means we don't need to consciously remember the steps to perform that task any more; we forget they exist, and soon can't recall them. This is unfortunate, because knowing the steps is absolutely essential if you want to teach anybody else how to do it.

Imagine you knew a basketball player who was amazing at getting the ball in the basket from a great distance. If you asked him how he did that, he would probably reply, 'I take the ball and I throw it like this.'

The problem is that lots of other people take the ball and throw just 'like this' and don't get it in, so what is he doing differently?

When you ask him to explain what he's doing differently, he'll probably just say something like, 'I don't know, I just do it.'

But if we want to learn how to be as good as him at this skill, this isn't much use to us.

So the tough news is that geniuses are brilliant at things many of us would love to be able to know how to achieve, but unfortunately tend to make the worst teachers, simply because they have forgotten the steps that we need to know.

The good news is that this is where NLP, the Lightning Process and this book come to your rescue, as they can help you to uncover those forgotten genius steps and then teach those steps to someone else.

One of the areas where the LP and this book differ from NLP is that with NLP you need an expert to help you, but with the LP and this book you can become the expert yourself and apply the skills at working out what steps will help you to be a genius at happiness and fulfilment. The above ideas can be summarized as 'if one person can do it then anyone can learn to do it too'. This is an empowering idea, but, as it's a big claim, it is sometimes met with the reasonable questions:

- Can it really be true that you can teach anybody anything?

- Or aren't some people just more talented at something than others?

There is some truth to this, as I'm certain that some people are born more talented than others in particular areas; Usain Bolt, the magically fast Jamaican sprinter, would be a good example. But it's important not to use this as an excuse as to why we can't do things, by stating 'this is just something I can't do,' or 'I simply don't have a talent for this.' Bear in mind that most people who have made outstanding achievements did so because they took their talents and worked on them. It's certainly been my experience over the last three decades that if we can learn some of the elements of how they got to be so good at something, we can emulate it to some degree or another.

The skiing gene

Only a few decades ago skiing was considered to be a genetically inherited talent because it seemed that only people who lived in remote mountain villages had the ability to ski. Often during the winter they were cut off from other villages and so the gene pool was quite small and the theory 'skiing is a genetic inbuilt talent' was further supported by the fact that people who didn't live in those villages seemed to be completely incompetent at skiing, no matter how much support and assistance they had from the villagers. But, as you should now know, asking a genius at skiing how to ski is the least effective way of learning this skill.

Nowadays the idea that the ability to ski is genetic seems ridiculous, but the only reason we now hold this new belief is because we've seen or experienced the benefits of an effective ski training based on a rational and systematized approach. So someone, somewhere, went through the process of breaking down the steps of skiing well enough to teach it to others.

So, you now can see that:

- The specific steps that make up a skill are identifiable.

- Geniuses have often forgotten those steps.

- If we learn the steps well enough we can replicate success.

- And teach it to others.

This leads on to the next lesson, which is all about a whole new way of looking at genius.

CHAPTER 4

Lesson 2: Upside-down Genius

One of the central ideas in this book is the absolute importance of taking a compassionate approach, which includes having

- Kindness and compassion towards our behaviours and ourselves.

- Kindness and compassion towards others and their behaviours.

- A readiness to assume any slights or misunderstandings were unintentional and a result of ineffective communication rather than malice, and to take responsibility to see things in the most healing light possible.

Virginia Satir, one of the great pioneers of family therapy, summarized this well when she said, 'Feelings of worth can flourish only in an atmosphere where individual differences are appreciated, mistakes are tolerated, communication is open, and rules are flexible – the kind of atmosphere that is found in a nurturing family.'

Adopting this compassionate frame of mind is of particular importance as we explore the extraordinary and unique ideas in the following section.

UPSIDE-DOWN GENIUS

As you learned in the previous chapter, I've been fascinated by genius for years and have looked for it for everywhere. As a result there is a whole list of genius behaviours that I've worked with, identified and broken down into their simple component steps.

But along this journey something struck me suddenly: if genius is defined as 'the ability to consistently reproduce the same results on demand, unconsciously', then there are whole bunch of other genius-level skills that I could add to my collection. And these next few ideas might just change the way you see yourself and life forever...

These special type of genius behaviours that caught my eye were when people were:

- Really great at something,
- But the results they were getting from doing that 'something', consistently and unconsciously,
- Were absolutely dreadful.

Just sit with that idea for a moment: that we could be brilliant at producing disastrous results in our lives – geniuses excelling at all the wrong kind of things.

Do you see where we're going with this?

I call these special kinds of genius behaviours 'Excellences of Limited Function', or 'ELFs' for short, and have found them in everyone, including myself, and especially those people who were very stuck. Suddenly, I started to see these people as geniuses, and as soon as I explained what's covered in this chapter, instantly they started to realize that they were geniuses too.

So let's look at a few very common examples of ELFs just to highlight the awesome power of this realization.

STRESS AND WORRY

Let's begin by taking the example of someone who is unfortunate enough to feel extremely stressed and worries endlessly. Normally that would never be considered to be the behaviour of a genius, but that misses an exciting opportunity for change. And with stress and anxiety becoming an epidemic in societies around the world, clearly the current solutions and theories aren't working too well.

Remembering that geniuses are unconsciously engaged in various thought processes, ask yourself the slightly strange question:

If I were to consider them to be a genius – somehow able to consistently and unconsciously reproduce the same results on demand – then logically, what results could I identify that they are consistently producing?

From this perspective, we can compassionately recognize that people experiencing high levels of stress and worry are somehow achieving some very specific and reproducible results, obviously without meaning or wanting to – remember genius is unconsciously competent. The unwanted and disastrous results they appear to be unintentionally 'excellent' at producing include:

- Being very good at imagining all the possible things that could go wrong.

- Considering all the solutions there would be to those problems, and what could go wrong with those solutions too.

If you take just a moment to consider anybody you know who is experiencing stress and worry, you can recognize that somehow they've developed the ability to completely perceive the world in this way, to genius level.

Once again let me emphasize, they are not 'doing it on purpose', as genius is unconscious. Certainly no one would want or choose to feel this way, no one would actively pursue these ways of thinking, and yet somehow that's exactly what they do. So much so, that when they are in a stressed phase, no matter what you try to do to calm them down, they have an uncanny ability to see instantly why that wouldn't work, as the following example demonstrates.

Super-safe room

If you ask someone who has severe stress to sit in a room, and then tell them all the reasons why this is the safest room in the whole world – 'The walls and floor are made of extra-thick reinforced concrete built to withstand earthquakes and explosions, the window panes are made of bulletproof glass, the air is imported daily from the Swiss Alps and all the food in the room has been blessed by the Dalai Lama' – do you think they'd feel comfortable and relaxed as a result of sitting in this specially designed room?

As you may have guessed, the answer is 'no'. They are instantly able to find reasons why that room will make them anxious. For example, they may wonder how they will get out of the room if there's an emergency, such as a fire at the doorway, and with all that reinforced concrete and bulletproof glass it sounds like it would be impossible to get out in any other way.

Their discomfort is due to their genius-level ability to think about problems. Even when there aren't any, they'll be able to convince themselves that this is just the calm before the storm; so when everything is good it's time to get very, very worried. Their genius seems to be that when things are bad they feel stressed and when things are good they feel stressed.

Again we can see the genius nature of this; somehow it has got so brilliantly designed that all situations and events lead to exactly and precisely the same outcome – stress.

In fact, I've met some people who are so good at ELFs (Excellences of Limited Function) that if 'being stressed' was an Olympic event, they'd definitely be on the team. Maybe you have friends who might get a place on the team, too? And, maybe, there would be a place on that team for some of you too?

As this is such a new and unfamiliar way of looking at things, it could be misconstrued as blaming the stressed people for being stressed. Just to be clear, that is not the message at all.

The person is not getting stressed about the super-safe room on purpose – it's an unconscious process that's making them feel this way. Nobody would want to feel stressed – it's not a conscious choice they're making; it's just something they've become very good at without even knowing how. But this fits exactly with our definition of genius, 'being really good at something while not really knowing how you are doing it, and so it seems to be happening all by itself.'

It's exactly the same answer as our imaginary basketball player gave when asked how he shoots hoops from such a distance: 'I don't know, I just do.'

From this we can start to see that if stress is an example of a kind of 'genius' creating a version of the world that is producing appalling feelings, what else could be seen in this way.

UNHAPPINESS AND FEELING DOWN

Let's continue to deepen our understanding of ELFs by taking the example of someone who feels unhappy or down much of the time. Normally, 'feeling down' would never be considered to be genius behaviour but, as with stress, this perspective opens new avenues for change.

Remembering if we were to compassionately consider them to be a genius – somehow achieving some very specific and reproducible results, obviously without meaning to or wanting to – then we can see that the unwanted and disastrous results they appear to be unintentionally 'excellent' at producing include:

- Hopelessness about the future

- Bleakness about the present

- Flatness about any positive experiences

- Immersion in any negative ones

If you take just a moment to consider anybody you know who is experiencing 'feeling down' then you'll recognize that somehow they've developed the ability to completely perceive the world in this way, to genius level.

Once again, I want to emphasize that they're not 'doing it on purpose' – genius is unconscious. Certainly, no one would want or choose to feel this way. No one would actively pursue this way of thinking; and yet, somehow, that's exactly what they do. So much so, that when they are in a 'down' phase, no matter what positives you show them to cheer them up, they have an ability instantly to perceive them as negatives.

The cake

Imagine you see a friend one morning and notice that they're looking a bit low, a bit flat, so you ask, 'How are you feeling?' and they reply, 'I'm feeling really down.' As their friend you're sorry to hear this so you hatch a plan to cheer them up.

You go away and bake a beautiful chocolate cake for them; you're hopeful this'll make everything better. But when you give them the cake, they look at you, and they look at the cake and they don't look happy. You ask them what's wrong and they say one of the following things:

'This is the worst thing you could have given me. When I'm upset I always eat too much and now there's a chocolate cake in my house that is just going to make everything worse. I wish you hadn't bothered.'

Or they might say, 'I really understand that you're trying to cheer me up with this cake, but I don't feel any happier, and that just makes me realize how fundamentally damaged I am, as I can't even feel happy or positive when somebody like you does something so generous. I wish you hadn't bothered, it's just made me feel worse.'

You leave their house feeling a little disappointed you weren't able to help them with your gift and decide to check in with them the next day.

When you arrive in the morning they still don't look happy. 'How are you feeling?' you ask once again. They reply, 'I feel dreadful. After you left I felt even lower, for the reasons I described yesterday, and then ended up eating that cake and now I feel unhappy and fat, which makes me even unhappier.'

This wasn't the result you wanted at all. It doesn't seem like being kind, positive and generous has made any difference. So if that didn't work, you reason, it's time to try the opposite approach of being firm.

You shake them by the shoulders, look them in the eye and tell them that they need to 'wake up and smell the coffee, to get a grip, to stop moaning, to realize the good things in life, because there are lots of them, and to just get on with it'. You're pretty sure this will do it, as being kind clearly didn't work.

So you're surprised when they just seem to look more upset. 'Well, it's just as I thought,' they say 'I knew today was going be even worse than yesterday and your unkind thoughtlessness has just proved it to me and shown me how bad life can be.'

In this scenario, it seems that no matter what you do, whether you're kind, firm, inspiring or just leave them alone, none of it makes any difference. You may have had this exact experience when trying to help your friend who's feeling down. If you try and cheer people up from their 'down feelings', it rarely works for any long period of time; if you try to shock, shame or motivate them out of it that rarely works either, and the reason why none of these things work?

Well, most useful way to see this is to realize that they are more of a genius at staying stuck (without meaning to be) than you are at helping them get unstuck. And naturally the person with the most genius will always 'win'.

Once again, to ensure there's no confusion over this, they are not doing it on purpose; it is not something they are consciously choosing to do, it's an unconscious behaviour they've developed and now it seems to run all by itself.

GUILT

It's also worth briefly stepping into the shoes of someone who has the Guilt ELF (Excellence of Limited Function). They have, somewhere along the line, developed an enormously brilliant ability to feel bad about things they should, or shouldn't, have done (according to their own or someone else's rules). They are such geniuses at this, and maybe you know someone like this,

PLAN A: **TAKE A COMPASSIONATE APPROACH.** THERE IS NO PLAN B.

that in those rare moments when they don't feel guilty about anything they may pause for reflection. In that moment, they suddenly realize they feel really guilty about the fact they're not feeling guilty about anything!

Once again, this is a great example of genius behaviour, where we get the same result regardless of what's going on around us.

What's the point of guilt?

Guilt has virtually no purpose whatsoever; we can see how people with the Guilt ELF are great at triggering it when they think they may have done something 'wrong'. The main problem is that it only leaves them with a sense of being wrong, but doesn't necessarily motivate them to change their behaviours or sort out any mess that needs resolving. And this is why it's a much overrated emotion – there is little value to be gained from wishing we hadn't done something a certain way, unless there is some kind of commitment to not doing it again.

The following story highlights the pointlessness of guilt.

<u>Guilt cabin</u>

Once upon a time, a young man was walking through some remote mountains, when suddenly the weather turned for the worse. As he struggled on through the driving snow, becoming colder and more concerned about how he was going to survive the night on the mountains, he was relieved to see dim lights ahead. Getting closer he saw the light was shining out of the windows of two very similar huts; one was left of the track and the other was on the right.

He suddenly realized where he was; these were the infamous residences of two strange men who, rumour had it, were both serial killers. He was left with a dilemma; stay out in the cold and freeze to certain death or spend the night in the company of one of the probable murderers.

As luck would have it, he chose to knock on the door of the house on the left. A huge bear of a man slowly cracked open the door. Peering at his unexpected visitor he asked. 'What do you want?'

'I am desperate to stay the night,' the boy shivered, 'but, and excuse me for asking, although I would like to stay the night I have heard unsettling rumours about you and the man who lives over there. I wonder if you could comment before I decide what I shall do about taking care of myself this evening?'

The huge man smiled, 'Come in for just a minute,' he said.

Extremely cautiously the young man accepted the invitation.

'Between you and me,' said his host, 'it is true I have killed many people. And I don't feel any remorse or guilt about it at all. In my mind, they were bad people and they deserved to die. However, I'm absolutely clear that this is something I will never ever do again, for now I'm a changed man and this is not part of my life. The man on the other side of the tracks has also killed many people; however, although he feels remorseful and guilt-ridden about it, he continues to do it. This is the uncomfortable truth. The question is: which house would you prefer to stay in? The one of the man who feels very bad about what he's done, but continues to do it; or someone like me, who is at peace with what they've done, but will never repeat those destructive behaviours?'

LOW SELF-ESTEEM

Few things are more crippling than having low self-esteem and interestingly its presence doesn't seem to depend on whether someone's achieved lots of success in life or not.

Self-esteem is only ever based on a measurement we've made about ourselves, and because we've made it we're always right about it.

For example, if someone tells us 'you have great self-esteem' when we don't feel it, then our self-esteem doesn't improve.

Equally, if we have great self-esteem and somebody says, 'You don't have good self-esteem' then we still feel we have good self-esteem.

This is due to the fact that only you can decide what level of self-esteem you have.

Reason for living

A few years ago I worked with an internationally acclaimed pop star. I hadn't seen them for a while, and when I asked how life had been going they replied, 'It's been the worst few weeks of my life.'

This seemed strange because their new album was critically acclaimed and was selling by the bucketload, and they'd flown to New York for a secret gig, which was a sell-out and received rave reviews. For most people this would be evidence of having a great month rather than the worst time of their life, so I asked what was making them feel so awful and with a sigh they replied:

'At the after-show party of the New York gig, a stranger turned up clutching my new album. They walked up to me and asked me to sign it. While I did, they told me something that made me decide to give up writing music and burn all my guitars.'

Can you guess what they said?

It wasn't, 'Your album and music stink,' or 'you're a horrible person' or anything like that. Instead, they said, 'I was about to kill myself, I couldn't see any point in living, my life was a mess, the future looked bleak. As I contemplated ending it all, I listened to your CD, and something in the music and the lyrics moved me, and I began to see that maybe I had got it all wrong, and there was a future, there was hope. And there and then I decided not to kill myself, and to make something of my future. Your music saved my life.'

Now, to me, this doesn't sound like the worst thing in the world that anyone could say. In fact, if you're a musician, surely it's one of the best things you could hear.

But this musician was a genius at low self-esteem (it was their ELF), at somehow being wrong about everything, and so they'd taken this positive comment and thought, *Well, I'm not a very happy person myself and, at some point, the story of my unhappiness will be spread across the tabloids, and this person will read that story. It will make them reappraise the album, knowing more about my personal unhappiness. They'll think about the lyrics and music in a new, bleaker way. And there's a good chance this will take them back into that dark space and they'll commit suicide. And it will all be because of me*.

Now, as this true story illustrates, that *is* quite a turnaround; to move from one of the best things anyone could ever say to you, and to make it feel like you're the worst person in the world. That's true genius, not good, or very useful, but certainly extraordinary.

Exercise: ELF Spotter

Complete this exercise to help check your understanding of ELFs (Excellences of Limited Function) before moving on.

- What have you learned now about the nature of genius?
- What is an ELF?
- Now you know about ELFs, who do you know who is a genius at an ELF?

Here are some ideas to get you started; maybe you know some people who are amazing at:

- Seeing how the night you've planned for them is going to turn into something very tedious or go wrong.
- Seeing the flaws in others.
- Finding something to disagree about.
- Finding something that is stopping them from being happy.
- Making things more complicated.

- Finding someone else to blame that stops them making changes themselves.
- Being cynical.
- Feeling disconnected.
- Finding something to moan about.
- Finding something to worry about.
- When you complement them, finding a part of their body/outfit to focus on that they don't like.

It's so easy to see these things in others but hey, if you're reading this book, there's a strong possibility that you're also a genius in an ELF or two. A number of the ELFs are listed on page xii, as reasons why you might be reading this book, and there's a whole range to choose from in the section above. But don't be limited to these ones; they're just the tip of the ELF iceberg. When you look at yourself, honestly, with a view to really making lasting change, which ones do you think you are best at doing?

CONGRATULATIONS!

You definitely deserve to congratulate yourself, because it turns out you are a genius, and this is brilliant news.

There's a very good chance you spent a long time being hard on yourself. Quite often, people feel a bit flawed, a bit broken, a bit like a piece is missing, and think that's why they're not as happy and fulfilled as they want to be. Actually, that's not the truth at all. You are complete and a brilliant genius already, it just so happens that some of the things at which you excel don't produce the results you want in your life. But that doesn't take away from the fact; you are a genius producing consistent and reliable results.

In my work, dealing with chronic illness and seriously life-threatening habits, this realization – that, actually, 'you're a genius, not broken or flawed' – has been pivotal to changing

41

those people's futures. So, allow yourself that recognition and congratulate yourself on being a genius too. You might as well take the praise; you've certainly put the work in getting this good at it!

The second thing you need to know about being a genius at a number of these ELFs is that it tells us a lot about you and the smartness of your brain. If you've been this good at producing these results then you have the ability to excel, as you have a well-functioning neurological system skilled at producing predictable results. All you need to do is get it to do something slightly different – and that's very simple.

GENIUS OF CHANGE

There are two phases to this process of change. First, you need to learn how to fail at being a genius at the things you're currently very good at, the ELFs, and learning to fail at achieving a goal is very easy. For example, imagine you're excellent at spelling but in order to help your friend to get the girl of his dreams you need to lose the spelling competition so he can win and get her attention. If you choose to help your friend in this way simply adding a 'Z' to every word will ensure your spelling results are very poor. You can see from this how easy it is to change once you've decided to no longer be a genius at something. Second, once that brilliant neurology is no longer reserved for your ELF, you can use it to achieve a more life-enhancing goal.

You'll see, many times over, that much of your brain doesn't really think much about what it does, it only does what it has been trained to do. Knowing this section of your brain's pathways is so good at getting results means it will be child's play to get what you want. If you think about one of your ELFs and consider how amazingly good you've been at producing that result; how consistent, how creative you've been in getting that result without even thinking, then you know you've got a very powerful ally on your side. An ally so determined, motivated and effective that when you can harness it to your new goals the results are certain.

Exercise: Acknowledge your genius

Review this chapter and get completely familiar with the idea that you really are a genius and it's time to put that genius to good use.

Now complete these sentences, with as many answers as come to mind: most people are geniuses at more than one ELF (yes, you're multitalented!)

1. I now see I've been a genius at...
2. If I were to harness that unconscious genius ability, that extraordinary machinery, and put it to some other use then...

   - What would I throw all that genius energy and neurology into?
   - How great would I be at that new behaviour?

Now that you recognize you **are** a genius, we're ready to move on to making some changes, so that you can get the life you love.

CHAPTER 5

Lesson 3: The Recipe of Genius

In the previous chapters we looked at how we learn something and how this can lead to us becoming a genius at it. Now we are going to take the next logical step and consider how we make changes to the things we've learned that are getting in the way of living the life we love now. Our first stop on this journey is to understand the steps in the recipe for being a genius. And we're going to do that by looking at how to bake chocolate cake.

The structure of success

Imagine you wanted to learn how to make a chocolate cake really well. To begin with you'd probably start off with a recipe, and the recipe would go something like this:

1. Select your ingredients (this will include flour, butter, eggs and sugar).

2. Add cocoa powder.

3. Mix the ingredients together.

3. Bake in the oven for specified time.

With practise and experience you could become a genius at making chocolate cake. But then, once you've mastered cake baking, someone decides to play a practical joke on you by replacing the cocoa powder with an identical-looking tin of chilli powder. When you bake the cake this time, because of the substitution, you'll naturally get a completely different result – a chilli cake.

The next day you buy new cocoa powder, but while you're out the prankster, who was very pleased with the results yesterday, decides to swap your oven for your dishwasher. They do such a brilliant job of this that you don't notice (they are a genius at this kind of thing). So when you bake your cake in the dishwasher instead of the oven, again you get a very different result to what you expected.

Realizing the appliances have been swapped you then spend the rest of the day rearranging your kitchen, and tired out, go to bed. As you sleep the prankster sneaks into your kitchen, takes down the book from the shelf and rearranges the order of the recipe so that now the recipe reads:

1. Select your ingredients (this will include flour, butter eggs and sugar).

2. Bake the ingredients individually.

3. Mix the ingredients together.

4. Add cocoa powder.

Again, this is going to give us a very different result.

Changing just the smallest element, like the chilli for the chocolate, of the standard recipe for making a cake radically changes the outcome.

The cake's success is dependent upon the recipe's structure, so we have to ensure we:

1. Do the right things.

2. In the correct way.

3. In the correct order.

Stray from these three rules and you **will** get a different result.

ELFs (Excellences of Limited Function) work in exactly the same way. They are dependent on a very particular precise structure; you have to do the right things, in the right way, in order to get the exact result you're expecting.

Again, this comes back to the definition of genius as being:

- Reproducing
- The same results
- On demand

You can only get the same results if you're consistent in using the same steps each time to achieve them.

If we take the old adage[3], the definition of insanity is 'doing the same thing time and time again and expecting to get different results,' then we can recognize that, if you want to get different results, you need to do something differently.

In the same way that a tiny change turned the chocolate cake into a chilli cake, equally the ELFs change massively, as a result of changing a tiny, single element of their recipe. In fact, that tiny change makes them fall apart, so they no longer function at the genius level. Also, as soon as we recognize they have structure, we become consciously aware of them. This moves them away from working very competently at an unconscious level to being something we can be very aware of at a conscious level; and there's an amazing amount of power to be gained through this shift of awareness.

Before, it appeared as though the ELFs just seemed to run on their own, to be slightly crazed ways of thinking, but when we recognize them as, first, genius behaviours and, second, as having a clear structure, we start to get a sense that these are not random events; they are clearly identifiable, reliable systematic 'machines' designed to produce one particular, brilliantly disastrous, product.

As soon as the ELFs are 'uncloaked' in this way, much like unmasking a swindler or seeing through a magic trick, we can see them for what they are and that insight allows us to break their hold over us.

The key thing to remember is ELFs have a structure. If you change the structure you'll get a different result, but it doesn't have to be a huge change – in fact any tiny change will do it.

IF YOU WANT TO
GET DIFFERENT RESULTS
YOU NEED TO
DO SOMETHING
DIFFERENTLY.

ONE OF THE SHARPEST TOOLS IN THE BOX

In the next chapter I'll introduce an incredible powerful life-changing tool that, if you take it on, like many of the core concepts in this book, will absolutely revolutionize your life and view of the world.

This might sound unbelievable but I've seen people get their futures back, revolutionize their relationships, their success and happiness levels and so much more as a result of using this next tool.

It's so significant that it has an entire book dedicated to it, *Dû – Unlock Your Potential With A Word*, which I recommend you read to gain an even deeper understanding of it.

On learning about it, one well-respected medical researcher said they felt it was possibly the most significant advance in healthcare since antibiotics and, probably most surprising of all, this tool is... a verb, a 'doing' word.

CHAPTER 6

Lesson 4: Active and Passive

It may strike you as rather odd that a new verb could be so important that it would change lives, or even that a new one needed to be created at all. We are more familiar with new nouns, which are thought up to describe something not in existence before, for example a smartphone. A new verb doesn't just create a single item, however, it describes a whole new thing that humans do that hasn't been defined before, so I'll explain why I created it and discuss its significance as we go.

It all began while working with people who had become stuck in their lives. As I listened to them speak, I noticed that as a group they consistently used language in a very particular way, which I decided to call 'passive' for reasons that will become clear. 'Passives' aren't only found with people who are stuck though; you can hear them causing trouble everywhere.

Let me give you an example of a passive phrase: I am stressed about the economy.

The problem with this phrase is that it declares that the economy is **causing** their stress and although it may seem this way, linking these two things together creates enormous problems.

If, as suggested by the statement, the economy was really responsible for their stress then, until the economy changes, and that's something they can't individually influence as it is beyond their power to change, then they're destined to feel stressed. They will just have to wait until those circumstances, which are completely beyond their control, eventually improve. So speaking about it in this way makes them feel completely powerless to do anything about it, and while the economy remains problematic then, predictably, their stress levels will also continue. It is precisely due to this sense of powerlessness, this inability to make a difference, which comes from using this type of language, that I've named it 'passive language'.

Think of it like being a passenger on a bus. You don't drive or steer the bus, you have no control over how it deals with the traffic or road conditions; the passive casts you as just being a bystander, a victim character in the play of life, a person with no influence to change anything. And feeling powerless is one of the fastest routes to unhappiness and feeling unfulfilled.

But, in fact, it isn't actually true that you are powerless. It's not the world economy causing them stress. We know this because of all the people who aren't that bothered by the economy; so the economy cannot be *inherently* stress-making. In fact it is the person responding to the economy news and generating and creating stress. Once again, they're not doing this on purpose; they don't mean to, it is because they are a genius at being stressed in this very particular context.

Once I heard this passive way of talking often enough to see it was causing problems, it became clear that I needed to find a way to help them move from being very passive to their stress to becoming powerful once again and regaining their influence in a situation – or, as I called it, 'active'. You'll recall the importance of influence from Chapter 2 (*see page 9*), meaning recognizing the things you can make a difference to and then taking action to change them.

The way the example passive statement is constructed suggests that 'there just isn't anything we can do', that we have no possibility of influence. So, the first thing to do is to change this statement so that it's really clear that we can do something about it. This is where we use the new verb, the Dû.

It has a similar meaning to the familiar English verb 'do' but with some very precise differences. The dû specifically means that we are unconsciously involved in the creation of some way of thinking or feeling.

Let's use the dû in our stress/economy statement to show how it's used. It's inserted in this way: I am dûing stress about the economy.

The dû emphasizes that we are involved but unconsciously and unintentionally (that's why it has a 'û' in it). So, as we are not doing it on purpose, there is absolutely no blame attached; however, because we're influential and involved in the situation it means we can then change what happens next.

Compare how it feels when saying out loud, 'I am stressed about the economy' compared to 'I am dûing stress about the economy.'

Notice that as soon as you say it in this way you're able to recognize your unconscious and unintentional role in the creation of the stress and it suddenly opens up a brilliant window of opportunity you were probably unaware of before. If you are 'dûing stress' then it's optional and you could stop dûing that stress and do (consciously) something else. And this is the beginning of retaking the power back in your life.

From now on, start using this life-changing way of seeing the possibilities in the world. Changing every one of those stuck passive statements into active ones will throw open the doors wide to the life you love.

I WAS JUST BORN WITH IT

Occasionally, I've heard people say that, although they understand the concept of dû, it doesn't apply to them; and, for example, might say, 'I'm just someone who IS shy and was born with low self-esteem; it's part of my make-up.' To them, this seems to be a completely accurate account of their situation but, with a little sideways thinking, we can see it's not quite as accurate as it should be.

Imagine a two-month-old baby; it's 3 a.m. and the baby wakes and wants something. Noticing the early hour, does the baby think *Oh, it's a bit too early and, although I have needs, they're not really as important as anyone else's. I certainly wouldn't want to upset or inconvenience anyone with my demands or embarrass myself by drawing attention to myself?*

No. The baby knows it wants something; it may not even be clear what it is, but will yell until someone meets its demands. If what they are given doesn't meet with their exacting expectations, they will feel very free to express their dissatisfaction and yell further until something better is produced.

From this, it becomes clear that we aren't born with low self-esteem, shyness, guilt, embarrassment, etc. In fact, these are things we learned to dû and, as we practised them a lot, we became very good at them, which made us start to think that that was 'who we were', rather than just a set of well-rehearsed behaviours.

THE SERENITY PRAYER AND STATES

This topic is covered extensively in *Dû – Unlock Your Potential With a Word,* but to break it down simply, the brilliantly insightful serenity prayer suggests we need to:

- Have the courage to change the things we can change.
- Have the serenity to accept the things we cannot change.
- Have the wisdom to know the difference between those two.

Have you noticed that so much of the time we put our energy into trying to change things we cannot change; trying to be in charge of things that we actually have no influence over – and we put

BECOMING AWARE OF THE KINDS OF THINGS THAT HAVE KEPT YOU STUCK IS THE FIRST STEP TOWARDS CHANGE.

insufficient energy into changing the things that we can? This is part of the formula for an unhappy and unfulfilled life.

A friend told me that when she lost her bag containing her keys, phone, money, cards, etc., everyone around her said, 'Oh, you must be so worried and stressed.' However, she decided to use the dû to get a life she loved, and so replied, to their astonishment, 'What's the point in dûing stress about it? How on Earth would that help me find the bag?'

When you think about it, she's right. You've probably noticed that being stressed is the least likely thing to help you think clearly and so recall where you might have left a lost item.

STATES

When we are, or more precisely, dû, stressed, we activate certain parts of our neurology that quickly access anxious memories or predictions, and stimulate the release of various neurotransmitters and hormones. The simplest way to explain this is that it gets us into a particular 'state'. In this case, the state of stress and anxiety.

One of the interesting things about states is that it appears that we can't be in two opposite states at same time.[4]

Exercise: Opposing states

Take a moment to check this theory out.

Can you actually laugh hilariously, with genuine good humour, while being sad? Can you feel really deeply relaxed and anxious at the same time?

You can swap, sometimes rapidly, between these two states but can't maintain them both at the same time.

So, it appears to be a general rule that although we can stray into similar states quite easily, such as sad, angry etc., we can't be in two opposite states at the same time.

Getting yourself into, or more precisely dûing, the wrong state or mind-set, or stimulating the wrong part of your nervous system (e.g. anxious, unhappy, overwhelmed) is one of the most common things that we dû as humans that gets in our way of having happiness and a great life.

Just consider for a minute how often we dû the following:

When we're in a hurry and get stuck in traffic, what do we dû then? Frustration, anxiety, stress? These things are all more likely to cause us to crash, have an argument, get an ulcer, etc., and least useful in making the traffic move.

What if you could learn to stop dûing stress and instead start doing calm?

DÛ AND DO

With this brief introduction to the dû, I hope you have a sense of how, when you use it all the time, you reclaim your power.

For completeness, however, it's worth mentioning that there are occasions when the old style of 'do' should be used, as dû is reserved for when you're involved in creating states without thinking; for example, we use dû for dûing stress as it's an unconscious and unintentional process. However, if you then intentionally decide to make yourself calm then this is *doing* calm, as it's an intentional, conscious process.

Of course, with time and practice, you could just start to dû calm unconsciously; and then you'd be a genius at calm.

Exercise: States

As using the dû allows you to recover your options it's also the fastest way I've found to getting back into a more appropriate state or mind-set, or activating the most useful part of your nervous system.

You can start increasing your awareness of when you need to use the dû with this exercise.

Make a list of the 'bad' or 'unhelpful' states that you commonly get into.

Now take each one and rewrite them adding in the dû, following the structure of the examples below:

- 'I get sad' becomes 'I dû sad'.
- 'I was angry' becomes 'I dîd angry'.
- 'My boss made me annoyed' becomes 'My boss said some things, and then I dîd annoyed'.

What are some common signs that you've been dûing the wrong state? Choose from this list below and make a note of any other ones you recognize:

- Losing your sense of humour
- Feeling irritable
- Blaming
- Beating yourself up
- Wishing it was different
- Feeling powerless
- Feeling picked on
- Feeling that it's everyone else's problem
- Feeling everything is against you
- Feeling nothing can help
- Feeling sad for no reason

DÛ REVIEW

So to recap this very brief introduction to dû, anytime you're feeling stuck, feeling that there's nothing you can do about your situation, feeling powerless, feeling like a victim of circumstance, it is time to use the dû. The dû will open up a new possibility immediately for you each time. It will help you uncover the elements of the situation that you'd forgotten you had influence over. It will remind you that you are actively dûing that negative behaviour; that it's time to stop dûing that and become powerful again.

In our original scenario, 'I am stressed about the economy', we can see that although there's clearly little we can personally do about 'the economy', we have immense influence over the amount of stress we are dûing.

Using the dû to recognize where you've given away your power and reclaiming it back is the first step to change. There are also a number of other steps, which naturally follow from this position; however, in many cases, just recognizing this and reclaiming your power with the dû is often enough to turn things around radically.

Now, time for a reality check…

CHAPTER 7

Lesson 5: Reality

Common sense tells us that we all exist in the same universe with the same reality, yet we also know that everyone has their own different version of what's really going on in the world. For example, when it's snowing for some (e.g. skiers, kids, etc.) it's the best kind of weather while for others (e.g. drivers, sunbathers, etc.) the worst. The big problem with reality is that we all think we know what it is; we generally think that our reality is the only one that's correct and possibly it is the only one that actually exists. In this chapter we're going to explore how wrong those assumptions are, and how much trouble they cause us.

FILTERS

The best way to understand how we filter 'reality' is by using the simple exercise below – read the first step and follow it before going onto the next one.

Exercise: Filter for red

Step 1

Take a moment to go into a room that has something red in it. A good place would be the kitchen if you're near one; go in there in preparation for this exercise, throw the cupboard doors wide open, as that's normally where red things live. If you aren't near a kitchen then choose another room that has some red in it.

Now follow these instructions.

Take three seconds to gaze around the room, taking in everything you can see that is red, because in just a moment you are going to leave that room and recall accurately everything that was red. Then leave the room and when you're far enough away that you can't peek inside, write down a list of everything you saw that was red.

Don't worry if you didn't recall many, just one or two is absolutely fine, and shows your brain is working very well.

Step 2

The next step is even more interesting, as I'd like you now to recall all the things you saw that were blue or green, without going back to the room.

Funnily enough, this is much more difficult to do. Many people will have a near-perfect recall of all the red objects and yet fail to recall much of what was green or blue. Take a quick trip back into the room with red things in; the chances are you will find many blue and green objects. Although it appears that you missed out observing some of the objects in that room, it is again an excellent sign that your brain is working very well.

The exercise's instructions asked your brain to look for, or 'filter', red objects, which it did very precisely. It noticed all the things that were red and recalled most of them. In many cases, it will also have spotted things that were near red in the colour spectrum, such as orange and purple objects.

What's intriguing, however, is what your brain does with things that are not red. The blue and green objects, for example, are not seen, not recalled and, even more significantly, disappeared from reality. It's almost as if they are just not there.

In my office I have a blue table, and sitting underneath it, carefully positioned behind one of the thick blue legs, is a large red box. When people do this exercise, they always see the large red box but never recall the blue table or the blue leg, which partially blocks their view of the box. When they recall the red box, even though there was a portion they couldn't see due to it being obscured by the table leg, in their mind they see the entire box. They have somehow managed to delete the blue table leg, and replaced it entirely with red.

This is actually normal brain function as the brain does exactly what we ask it to do – focus on one particular thing and pay attention to it. It hasn't got time to pay attention to everything else, as it would be a waste of energy and brain-processing power. However, naturally this approach means that we completely miss things we're not looking for and yet remain convinced that we've seen the whole story. We'll cover this in much more detail later in the ELF (Excellence of Limited Function) recipes chapters (*see pages 263–294*) but to sum it up briefly:

- Whatever you're finding in your world is a result of what you're looking for.
- If you're finding red everywhere, even when there's lots of blue and green, it's down to your brain's brilliant filtering process.
- Equally, if you're finding unhappiness everywhere then you can be sure that a large part of it is due to the fact that your brain is following instructions to look for unhappiness everywhere.
- If you're finding stress everywhere then, again, it's because your brain is following instructions to look for stress everywhere.

Exercise: What are you looking for?

If it seems that you've got too much of anything negative in your life then spend a few minutes working out the answer to this question. Write down your answer.

- What have I been looking for?

OPTICAL ILLUSIONS

The 'filter for red' exercise above shows how we can *mis-see* reality, but it gets even worse, as these next simple but significant exercises demonstrate.

The magnifying box

Look at the text in the 'square surrounded by four circles' section.

Equally, if you are finding [obscured]ess [obscured]re, you can be sure that a large part of that is due t[obscured] fact the brain [obscured]lowing instructions to look for unhappiness everywhere. If you're finding stress everywhere, then again it's because your brain is followi[obscured] instructions [obscured] look for stress everywhere. So if it seems that you've got t[obscured]uch of anythi[obscured]gative in your life, spend a few minutes working out the a[obscured]this [obscured]: 'What have I been feeling lately?'

The words within the four black circles appear larger, clearer and as if there is a bigger space between the lines. But the text and line spacing is exactly the same as in the rest of the paragraph.

The Müller-Lyer illusion

Consider the lines below. Which is the longest?

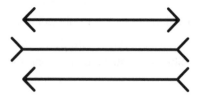

Well, it turns out, they're all the same length, as you can see from the illustration below.

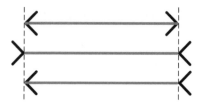

Interestingly, this illusion seems to work better in the Western world, which has created much debate. One set of data suggests this phenomena is related to familiarity with straight lines and angles due to most Westerners living in more 'regular-shaped' environments (e.g. most houses, cities, manufactured goods, etc. are based on straight lines and angles), so they are more used to the significance of lines and corners on dimensions.

Peoples such as the San who live in the Kalahari Desert, where straight lines aren't much of an environmental feature, are the least fooled by the illusion. Another set of data, however, suggests it might be due to the differing pigmentation of the light-receptive retina, which is dependent on ethnic origin.

Whichever theory turns out to be correct, both sets of data show that there is a variance of the extent to which people are fooled by the illusion, and this further supports the theme of this chapter – that there are so many versions of the same reality!

The Orbison illusion

Keen students of optical illusions will recognize the following illustration as a variant of the Hering illusion, discovered by the German physiologist Ewald Hering in 1861. The psychologist William Orbison first described this version, which I think is the best, in 1939.

As you look at the diamond shape in the middle of Figure 1, you'll notice it looks distorted; however, as you've probably guessed by now after a few of these illusions, it's not (Figure 2).

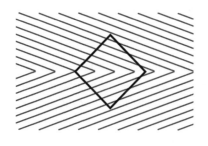
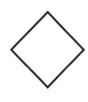

Figure 1   Figure 2

Hermman-Hering grid

Below is another of my favourites by Herr Hering. Count the black dots you can see at the intersections of the grey lines.

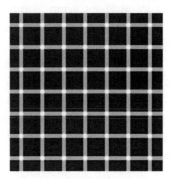

Most people find they can't count the black dots because as soon as you look at them they turn white. Some people find they can't even see black dots as they change to white so quickly. Again, both are normal brain functions. But when you can see black changing to white in front of your eyes (and remember our experience of looking for red and only finding red), you might want to stop for a minute and consider:

Do we really see anything as it truly is?

And if it is natural that we distort our perception of reality all the time and completely buy into that distortion as being how the world actually is, then it raises an interesting question. Maybe we should be more careful, more proactive and more selective about how we distort that reality, so that it actually serves us better?

THE GRAPH OF LIFE

When you look at most people's lives over a long enough period of time, you'll see ups and downs – everybody has a wide range of experiences. I think it's fair to say that there is a mixture of some great, good or mediocre things and some slightly negative, bad and quite dreadful things that occur in everyone's lives. And overall there is probably a fair balance of both positive and negative occurrences. Yet different people seem to have very different experiences of how great or appalling their lives are, but when you sift through their life's events it's difficult, objectively, to see that one life was better or worse than the other in terms of what actually happened. How can we explain this discrepancy between what actually happened and the genuine experience?

The following graph shows the relationship between events and time, and so helps to explain this very important fundamental of life:

Figure 1

In the above figure, the line follows a course through extremes of both good and bad. But an interesting thing can be observed of people who appear to be unhappy, or more correctly, people *dûing* unhappiness. They notice there are good times and bad times. But they especially notice that the good times are followed by bad times, which destroys and blocks out any of the good feelings created by those good times. This tells them that if a good time is occurring, then, sure as night follows day, a bad time is on its way to them.

As a result, they start to follow the graph shown below.

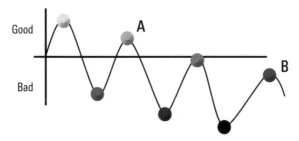

Figure 2: point A indicates that things are better for this person, but they are sure it won't be long before things turn bad again; point B indicates their experience that there's more bad than good.

Each time something good happens they destroy it by anticipating the inevitable descending gloom. Unfortunately, this has the effect of making each downward turn even darker and more depressing, and so making it much more difficult for any of the positive events that do occur to have any life-changing impact. As result, this encourages an increasing feeling that the world is full of bad experiences. When they look at their life it seems very clear to them that life is difficult and not much fun, and that's just the way it is. An external observer will notice that actual events in their life follow very much along the lines of the first graph (Figure 1) – an equal amount of good and bad – but to the person with (dûing) unhappiness their genuine experience is that life is fairly dreadful.

REAL-WORLD FILTERS

Let's take a break from that unhappy version of the world and instead imagine it's the day of the biggest event in the world of football (soccer), which only happens every four years – the World Cup Final, and you're playing for your country.

The game is about to end, there are only three seconds left, when your team is awarded a penalty. (For those who don't know the game, a penalty is when the ball is placed on a spot in front of the goal, and one player has the unenviable task of kicking it past the highly trained goalkeeper.)

Imagine that in this particular game you have personally scored 10 goals, while the opposition have scored none. Although there are many millions of people around the world watching you about to take this penalty kick, it's fairly irrelevant whether you get it in or not: your team is going to win either way and, if you win the World Cup and have scored 10 goals in the final, you will be considered a living legend. People will name their children after you; buy you drinks in any bar for rest of your life and your name will be added to the roll-call of heroes. Getting it in would be nice, of course, but it's not really that important if you do or if you don't.

So, as you step up to take that penalty, how do you imagine you would feel?

Probably quite calmly confident, excited by the fact that this is a chance to score the 11th goal and knowing that within a few short seconds you and your teammates are going to be raising the World Cup and celebrating. What would you imagine are the chances of successfully getting your shot past the goalkeeper?

The answer is it's probably fairly high, around about 70–80 per cent?

However, let's imagine a slightly different situation. It's still the World Cup Final, again there are only three seconds left on the clock and your team is awarded a penalty. However, this time, you and your team haven't scored any goals so far and, even worse, the opposition is currently winning with one goal. Now this penalty kick becomes very significant. If you get it in you will have levelled the scores – a heroic feat. As the final cannot end in a draw and someone has to win, the game will go on to a period of extra time. It will be tiring but at least you have created the possibility of scoring a goal in extra time and winning the World Cup.

If, however, you fail to get your shot past the goalkeeper, the final whistle will be blown, the game will end, and you and your teammates and your country will lose. Now in every bar you go into, every TV appearance you ever make, some mention will be made of the moment you personally lost the World Cup.

As you step up to take this penalty, how does this version of the same event feel?

Probably you'll be fairly stressed and quite concerned about the outcome. What would you imagine the chances of getting your shot past the keeper are this time? It's probably quite a lot less than before, maybe 30–40 per cent?

Interestingly, in the highest levels of football and many other sports, there is a group of performers who are able to score with a 70–80 per cent hit rate in the first scenario. What makes them so special is that they are also able to score with exactly the same 70–80 per cent hit rate in the second scenario – the one where they are losing and all the pressure is on them.

They somehow put themselves in a position where, in spite of whether they're winning or losing at this point in time or whether this particular kick is a game/life-changer or not, they're able to perform brilliantly. They define genius, they are being their best; replicating the same results on demand, unconsciously, independent of what's going on around them (see Figure 3).

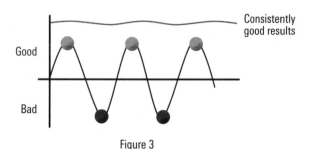

Figure 3

Some of the key elements of how they do that include telling themselves, quite reasonably, that:

- I am among the most highly trained people in the world at doing this.
- I am good at this – this is what I get paid for.

They remind themselves that in both scenarios the ball is the same shape and the goalkeeper is just as prone to human error. They are also able completely to blank out the rest of the universe and keep their focus entirely on the ball and where it is going to end up. Nothing else exists for them in that moment; they are geniuses at filtering in a really useful way.

Naturally, if you were choosing players for your international team, you would much prefer to have people like this who were able to score when they're winning and when they're losing rather than just those people who were able to perform at their best only when they're winning and everything's going in their favour. I would like you to pause for a minute, knowing what you now know about geniuses and filtering, and answer the following question.

Exercise: Genius perspective

What if you were able to take that same perspective as those football players? Deciding that you're the same 'you', independent of what's going on around you. Deciding to be your absolute best when it's easy to do that, as the world seems to be smiling on you, but also when everything seems to be against you. If you could do that in your life, in the same way as they do on the pitch, then what kind of extraordinary life would you start to attain? Make sure you record your responses in your workbook.

- My life would be... [*complete the sentence*].
- It would change in these four ways.

This outcome is exactly what you'll be learning to achieve throughout this book.

Now, you may not have noticed it before but that footballer and your route to happiness are very closely linked to a surprising creature, the rubber duck.

This unlikely hero explains a concept, which is core to osteopathy and many other alternative and complementary health approaches, and is vital to understand and embrace if you want to get the life you love – the rubber duck's ability to float.

Rubber duck

When 29,000 rubber ducks broke free from a cargo ship in 1990 and slipped overboard they became the unwitting participants in a survey of world weather patterns by oceanographer Dr Curtis Ebbesmeyer. He realized he was able to track the movements of this brightly coloured flotilla throughout the world by encouraging beachcombers to collect the ducks when they landed and send in their reports of sightings to him. By studying the ducks' adventures he was able to collect data about the oceans currents and changing weather patterns and so build a better model of how the complex system of worldwide ocean currents work. After 10 years at sea they had covered 17,000 miles, and now, 20+ years on, they are still exploring the world.

So imagine your surprise if you were to visit a swimming pool and as you gazed down into the depths of the clear water you noticed that there, submerged deep underwater, was one of our intrepid – and fundamentally buoyant – rubber duck adventurers. What is going on – we know that the rubber duck is unsinkable so why is it stuck deep under the water?

If you were to swim down you would find out that either something was getting in its way, blocking its passage back up to the surface, or that something was tying it down to the bottom of the pool. Once you'd worked out what the obstacle was and removed it, then the duck would naturally bob back up to the surface of the water. And, since its buoyancy is unchanged by time, it wouldn't really matter how long it had been submerged since it will rush to the surface as soon as it is set free.

Apart from not having beaks or being yellow we have a great deal in common with the intrinsically buoyant duck. My experience is that we have similar buoyancy, but ours isn't about an ability to float on water, ours is the inbuilt predisposition to soar on life's currents, to naturally bob back up to the surface of life and bask in the sunshine as soon as the storm has passed. We have a buoyancy of happiness, fulfilment and contentment – that's where we should be in life.

We also have within our genetic make-up the mechanisms designed to ensure we are vital, energetic, self-repairing organisms. It's a natural function of being one of evolution's winners; it's part of our blueprint to be radiantly healthy and to mount effective responses to illness and injury.

So while the duck has the inbuilt ability to float, we have the inbuilt ability to float right back up to being happy, fulfilled and healthy, and to feel great and intrigued about life. This is our normal – our birthright; anything else that we put up with as being

WE HAVE THE **INBUILT**
ABILITY TO FLOAT
RIGHT BACK UP TO
BEING **HAPPY, FULFILLED**
AND **HEALTHY,** AND
TO **FEEL GREAT** AND
INTRIGUED ABOUT **LIFE.**

the 'best we can get' denies the amazingness of what it is to be human. Not a robotic human defined by our past, our experiences, our childhood or parenting, but a vibrant being that is present to the possibility that we can write our future on a completely clean slate, that we can be the architects of what happens to us next and design a life we love, right now.

If you've learned to believe anything else other than this about yourself, then remember the duck: it is only held down temporarily. As soon as it's released it goes right back to where it should be, on the surface, basking in the sunshine.

And there's so much more to you than the limited one-trick rubber duck! You come equipped with the most highly developed processing system on the planet, the human brain; you are a member of arguably the most successful species the world has ever seen, so if you've forgotten how amazing and resilient you are, then it's time to take a moment to remember your true nature…

11-month-old you

Most people learn to walk at about 11 months. But it's not a simple, or initially successful, process. It was a long, protracted series of failures, of falling over and being beaten by gravity. But you didn't give up, in spite of the bruises and disasters, you just continued until you mastered it.

This is who you are – a succeeder, someone who expects to overcome obstacles, who demands amazing experiences and keeps going until they get them. With that history alone you owe it to yourself to make sure you don't sell yourself short for anything less.

THOUGHTS AND REALITY

Clearly, there is a link between our ways of thinking and what we perceive as reality, so we need to explore the nature of those thoughts by answering this interesting question:

What happens to your thoughts when you're not thinking them?

So if you have an anxious thought and then you think about something else, what happens to that anxious thought when you're not thinking of it?

There tends to be two schools of thought about how to answer this question.

The first, and most common, is that when we are not thinking them, our thoughts hang around in our unconscious or they are still there quietly operating, waiting for their chance to jump back into the foreground of our mental focus.

The second perspective theorizes that when we are not thinking some specific thoughts, then they do not, in that moment in time, exist.

Which one do you buy into?

My experience is that the second perspective is much more accurate and useful. It's more accurate because, as we should recognize having studied active and passive language earlier (*see page 51*), thinking is an active process. Thoughts are therefore a shorthand description of that active process. If we are not thinking in a particular way then we will not be actively creating those thoughts, and so for that moment in time those thoughts don't exist. And this is even easier to see if you substitute the idea of 'dance' for 'thoughts'.

If I perform a beautiful dance and afterwards you're so impressed that you ask where I keep my dance when I'm not dancing, and whether you can purchase it or borrow it, then we can clearly see that this makes no real sense as a question. The dance doesn't have that kind of existence; it's not an object or thing, it's an action process, which only exists while we are activating it. Once we stop dancing a particular dance there is no more dance. And so, when we stop thinking a particular thought there is no more of that thought, until we start thinking it again.

So, for example, until I mentioned it, were you thinking about a purple octopus eating strawberry and lemon ice creams? I am pretty certain that you weren't, but that you are now. (By the way, how many ice creams were there?) Where was that thought before you read that sentence? I think you'd agree that it didn't exist. When you read the sentence you activated the nerve pathways that created the idea of the octopus eating ice cream, and at that point the thought was generated. When I ask you instead to focus on the big toe of your left foot, then the 'octopus eating ice cream' thought is replaced by the new thought about your 'big toe'.

While it's true that we may have 'memories' of previous or past thoughts, they only really become thoughts when we reactivate those memories. Our brain just can't focus on all the memories we have of every single moment of our life all the time, it simply doesn't have the capacity to do that.

So when we are experiencing a 'thought' it is a choice that we are making somewhere to trigger and activate certain parts of our brain. This is good news because this means we are in charge of our thoughts…

Although, of course, in reality that is so rarely true. We may indeed be activating our thoughts, but we mainly don't choose which ones to activate consciously – again we see the power of the dû here. We are actively stimulating neurological pathways and generating thoughts (dûing thoughts), but we're so often doing it unconsciously, triggering 'bad' or un-useful and, very often, extremely familiar thoughts, which produce unpleasant feelings.

THOUGHTS AND FEELINGS

That last sentence illustrates why thoughts are so important to explore; our feelings don't arise for no reason or descend on us 'out of the blue', in spite of what many people will tell you. Feelings are a response to how we are seeing/thinking about the world and our current situation. The following story demonstrates this in action.

On/off

Imagine you're stressed and anxious about an interview next week. Suddenly an old friend, whom you haven't seen for years, calls out of the blue. You're so excited to hear from them, you get lost in the conversation and, as you talk, what happens to your stress levels?

They go down.

Until?

Well, either until you put the phone down, or maybe until that moment when you notice you're not stressed any more, which immediately makes you think about what you were stressing about before and reactivates the thoughts about the interview and the stress feelings.

Also imagine you go to work one day and have a really productive, great day. But when you get home you discover the washing machine has leaked and there's a mess to clean up. You might be irritated about it but notice, even though the leak may have been dripping all day, the earliest point you could get those irritated feelings is when you first find out about the leak – up until then, since you didn't know about the leak, you're just not activating 'there's a leak' thoughts, (unless of course you've been anticipating such an event – and planning that kind of thinking in advance - and as you are a genius, that's entirely possible!).

So, we can see how our attention switches in and out of those 'thoughts' (dôes thinking on and off), and the feelings flow with it. To summarize this important realization:

- Thoughts are the result of an active process that we are engaged in (as opposed to 'I have these thoughts', we can be more accurate and say, 'I am dûing these thoughts').

- Therefore we have the potential to regain charge of whichever thoughts we're choosing to activate.

- Since feelings are the result of our thoughts, changing our thoughts will change our feelings.

- If we want to lose our sense of unhappiness and lack of fulfilment then actually there is less to do than imagined. We need to begin by finding a way to stop the thoughts we're currently dûing and create new ones that become stable and dominant and our new default setting.

After all, if you learned to walk against the odds and have the resilient quality of a rubber duck, but find yourself in an unhappy, unfulfilled state, then you know this is not natural to you; it's something you've learned and something you can unlearn, and replace with some ways of thinking that move you towards a life you love.

RECAP
Before reading on, check you understand these vital topics:

- The presence and power of filters.
- That there are an infinite number of realities to choose from.
- That you are naturally resilient and buoyant.
- That your thoughts are the result of an active process.
- That your thoughts create feelings.
- That you can choose your thoughts, and decide how you feel about things.

Now you're ready to make sense of my in-depth research into the ELFs.

CHAPTER 8

Lesson 6: Genius Remembered

This chapter introduces a more in-depth approach to ELFs (Excellences of Limited Function). It's the result of talking to thousands of people with a genius ability to create disaster in their lives without even wishing/wanting to, and answering the question:

Exactly how did you dû that, without even thinking?

Once again, keep in mind that these recipes represent the unconscious sets of processes that the nervous system is going through. But almost 100 per cent of the time, in 100 per cent of cases, they're not doing it on purpose. They're not doing it to cause trouble or seek attention and not even doing it, as some psychologists sometimes suggest, for secondary gains (to get some benefit by doing it). They are running these recipes without even thinking; it took hundreds of hours of discussions with these ELF geniuses to even work out between us what must be going on to produce these results.

Once I'd initially identified some common patterns and themes with a few people experiencing that issue, the next step was to talk to hundreds of other people with the same issue and find out if they were doing the same thing or not. This allowed me to start to identify what was common to everybody with that issue.

So my purpose here is to identify the common factors and see that the issue, like the chocolate cake, has a recipe or blueprint (*see page 45*), then we can work out what to do to change it, to mess it up, so the pattern just can't run any more.

I worked on documenting the structure of many different core issues, through this process of discussion and research. I am not going to present all of these in this book; instead I am going to work in depth through four of the common ELFs that most easily show you how to apply these ideas to other issues in your life. These are:

- Low self-esteem
- Unhappiness
- Stress
- Guilt

Each issue is quite detailed, so 'low self-esteem' is covered in the next chapter, but the others are found in the appendices at the back of the book (*see pages 263–294*).

However, the next chapter is a **must-read** chapter, as it goes through each element of an ELF in even more detail. The other three chapters will then deepen your understanding of ELFs and are essential reading if they concern issues you're currently experiencing in your life.

If your issue doesn't quite match any of these, then take the role of a researcher and ask yourself:

What could be going on that would make me approach the world in this way?

Go through the headings listed in the ELF chapters and fill in the details. Consider how you deal with things and, as you've probably come across others with similar issues (possibly some who were even better at it than you!), also think about how they must be dealing with the world too, to get the results they got.

If you do have one of the ELFs listed on page xii, then start to work through it by comparing your experience to the general steps given in the relevant chapter.

STRESS, GUILT, UNHAPPINESS, ETC. ARE ALL BEHAVIOURS: SOMETHING WE DÛ RATHER THAN WHO WE ACTUALLY ARE.

In my experience, you should find that most, if not all, of the steps reflect accurately how you think about the world and how your brain operates. If there's a part of the recipe that you don't agree with, I'd suggest looking at it a little longer and seeing if it fits with you or not. It is possible that it isn't how you approach the world due to the fact that, of course, we're all a bit different. But mostly I find there is a very strong correlation between people having these feelings in their lives and approaching the world in the way described in the recipes.

Notice, naturally, the ELFs will only run in those times when you're thinking in this way, along the lines of the recipe. Because these ELFs are behaviours, something we **dû** rather than **who** we actually are, they are not always present. In those times when you're not dûing those feelings of unhappiness, you will also notice that those are the times when you're not running the patterns in the Unhappiness ELF recipe.

Also remember, as with the chocolate cake recipe (*see page 45*), if you change, mess with or miss out any one of the parts of the recipe then you get a completely different result. With the ELFs it's exactly the same. I'll be highlighting some elements of the recipe when it's so clear that changing this step would result in the whole ELF failing to work any more, but it's actually true of any step in the process.

I've written these from the perspective of what you would have to do in order to create brilliant genius levels of the problem. It's a kind of an upside-down way of looking at it but, by thinking in this way, it makes it easy to really see it as a skill. If you took anyone and asked them to start to approach the world in these very particular ways and they actually did it, it's pretty obvious they would produce powerful, reproducible, yet disastrous, results.

So if this is what you've got in your life, remind yourself that you are a genius and take a good look at what's been going on inside your brain behind your back; if the results hadn't been so negative on your life, it would be almost funny to finally see it in this way.

CHAPTER 9

Lesson 7: How to Be Even Better at Low Self-esteem

The term 'low self-esteem' is often used by psychologists but is, perhaps, less familiar in everyday conversation. It means exactly the same as low self-confidence or lack of self-belief and often shows up as shyness, embarrassment or being uncomfortable either in the company of unfamiliar people or when asked to perform or stand out in some way. For ease, I am going to use the term 'low self-esteem' to include all of these ideas and behaviours. As mentioned on page 80, this is a **must-read** chapter, even if you don't experience low self-esteem, as it will show you how to understand the structure of an ELF (Excellence of Limited Function).

RECOGNIZING THE LOW-ESTEEM ELF

Armed with your knowledge from the previous chapters, you'll understand what I mean when I say:

'In order successfully to dû low self-esteem you must dû the following things. It simply will not work properly if you don't.'

Let's look through the recipe that creates the genius of the Low Self-esteem ELF – you could use it to teach people how to be even better at low self-esteem (although I wouldn't advise it) – but mainly we'll explore how easy it is to fail at being a genius at it.

Step 1: Filter

You remember the 'filter for red' exercise (*see page 61*) where looking for red objects made red things show up?

In each ELF recipe, instead of looking for red, we become brilliant at looking for something very specific – which is different for each recipe. Again, naturally, when we look for these things they show up too.

So, in the recipe for low self-esteem it's important to set our filter to:

1. Look for more evidence of how:

    » Worthless, wrong or bad we are.

    » We always get it wrong.

    » We don't deserve good things.

    » Any success can be explained away as either 'easy to do anyway', the result of someone else's action or just random chance events.

    » We are less good than others. There is a sense these people are 'better than me'.

2. Anticipate that we're going to get it wrong, mess up, let others down or make a fool of ourselves.

Exception filter

However, there's an interesting added twist, called the 'exception filter', which comes into play whenever 'things seem to be going right', in spite of our negative predictions. This presents a real danger to the stability of our ELF and our negative feelings. But the ELF is so well designed that it has a built-in protection mechanism for situations such as these. It works in this cunning way:

As soon as it spots 'things seem to be going right' it convinces us that, as we are certain to mess everything up with an error very soon, this sense of 'everything is okay' is simply a temporary illusion.

Deluding yourself into believing 'everything is okay' will only mean that, when it all goes wrong, it will make everything seem even worse. We will have set ourselves up for such a fall that it might possibly totally destroy us. As a result, this news that 'things seem to be going right' doesn't stand a chance – it doesn't make us feel comforted or reassured at all.

Here's the filter in a handy table for quick reference:

Pattern	Single event	Creates prediction	Filter
Low self-esteem	A challenge arises	I'm going to get it wrong again; it'll just reconfirm how bad I really am; someone else would do it better	Everything I do always turns out bad because of my shortcomings

Exercise: ELF check

Do you sometimes use any of the above filters?

Yes/No

When you dû that does it get you a life you love?

Yes/No

Remember, these are things you dû, so there will be some times when you aren't dûing them; naturally, in those times, you won't experience low self-esteem.

The power and fragility of the ELF

We can see how having this way of interpreting the world, and these expectations of the future, will easily and rapidly create a spiral of low self-esteem. Good experiences can't get a foothold or exist for any period of time before being quickly extinguished.

The 'exception filter', in particular, is an extremely effective way of keeping us stuck. It's so well designed it destroys any glimpses of evidence that might disagree with the ELF's fundamental perspective that everything we do turns out bad, or that we are bad and wrong.

However, in spite of its powerful appearance, the ELF is fundamentally a fragile, easily exposed con trick.

Exercise: Failing at the ELF

Notice what happens when you consider what would naturally result from swapping these filters, and instead:

1. You looked for more evidence of:
   - How great you are and how you're always trying to do the right thing.
   - How you mostly get it right, try your best and do deserve good things.
   - How your successes were, at least partly, as a result of your own effort.
   - How you are as good as others, the sense that everyone is 'my equal'.
2. You anticipated that you were going to do your best, excel and make a positive difference.
3. You had the opposite 'exception filter'. You would expect things to go well and if ever things seemed 'a bit off track' you knew this was going to be a temporary situation. You'd see it as a sure sign you were heading somewhere – challenges are a sure sign of growth and new experience, which will deepen your sense of personal strength. You know that the sense of achievement you will get at the end of this will seem even better having weathered this storm.

What would happen if you were to take on this new set of filters and applied them with exactly the same amount of determination and consistency as those old low self-esteem filters?

You'd get a similarly powerful, but very different experience of the world and yourself. And this is the secret of success. Fail to be a genius at any one element of the ELF and, just like the illusion of the Emperor's new clothes, it will simply disintegrate in front of your eyes, stop working and you won't be able to take it seriously any more.

Step 2: Edit, distort and connect in problematical situations

This describes the ability we all have to brilliantly amplify how extremely challenging a problem is by beginning to edit out all types of events that don't fit or agree with a particular point of view we have.

Editing has a whole chapter later in the book (*see page 249*) but, for the moment, consider it to be a bit like coming home from a trip and looking through the photos you've taken, separating out the great shots from the dreadful ones and then throwing away the good ones and keeping the bad ones. As a result of that kind of editing process, it now appears from the photos you possess that either you are consistently appalling at taking photos or everything and everyone you saw was blurred, badly lit, or un-photogenic.

When we do this with our memories, selecting all the worst ones and ignoring the great ones, it creates a vast library of apparently similar events that seem to join up together and accurately represent the whole of our past.

This distorts our reality to make it appear that this problem occurs a lot, or maybe all of the time and gives it a sense of permanence, complexity and enormity that it doesn't really deserve.

Language

Once again, it's really worth listening to the language you use, as that's your first clue that you've become unintentionally involved in this kind of self-deception. When we are 'editing, distorting and connecting' we'll hear ourselves making generalized statements about things, or expressing beliefs that limit our view of the world. These will suggest that the world is one particular way, when, if we stopped to listen to ourselves for a moment, we'd know what we'd said wasn't entirely accurate. Generalizations and beliefs are, in most cases, very harmful and the basis of all bigotry, racism, sexism and any other -isms, but can easily be spotted by listening out for words such as:

- Every time
- All
- Never
- Always

- Each time
- As usual
- Forever
- Nobody, no one, etc.

These words (technically called 'universal quantifiers') help to suggest that this one event is part of a larger series of events, which always happen 'this way'.

Low self-esteem generalizations
What we actually say varies from ELF to ELF, but for low self-esteem it works really well to say things like:

- 'Every single time I try to do anything I **always** make a mess of it.'
- 'I **never** get it right.'
- 'I said the wrong thing, as **usual**.'
- 'Because I was involved it naturally went wrong, just like it **always** does.'

Exercise: ELF check

Do you sometimes find yourself using these kinds of ways of thinking or speaking?

Yes/No

When you dû that does it get you a life you love?

Yes/No

SPOTTING **CERTAIN WORDS** WILL BE YOUR **FIRST CLUE** TO THE PRESENCE OF AN ELF **(EXCELLENCE OF LIMITED FUNCTION).**

Failing to use the ELF

As you learn the tools in this book you'll become a genius at turning these kinds of patterns around. For now, notice how quickly the following technique highlights these ways of thinking and rapidly changes how you see things.

Exercise: Never?

Every time you hear one of these universal quantifiers just repeat it to yourself in a questioning way. Do this by raising your voice slightly at the end of the word while raising your eyebrows.

So, in the example, 'I **never** get it right', follow this by the questioning phrase, 'Never?'

Suddenly it all becomes clear that you don't actually buy into the version of the world you've been selling to yourself. Once again, we can see that any shift away from the basic steps of the recipe will mean the ELF falls apart.

Step 3: Step into nasty; step away from nice

There's a very simple rule in functional neurology, which is if you wish to have a more powerful emotional experience of a memory, you need to trigger as many of the nerve pathways that are connected to the original memory as possible. As we obviously experience the world fully immersed in our body's sensations, recalling it in that way will trigger the strongest response and feelings. Recalling an event in any other way, for example, distanced, as an observer or with some perspective, will produce a less emotional or powerful impact. The short way to remember this is:

- Stepping into a feeling and reliving it increases it – steps it up.
- Being out of it and observing it decreases it – fades it out.

In a similar way to the 'filters' of step one and the 'editing' of step two, step three of every ELF recipe deepens our experience of the 'bad' side of the world/life by getting us to immerse ourselves in 'bad' thoughts and states and distancing ourselves from the 'good' ones.

With practise, and the brain rewiring process of neuroplasticity, we can become amazingly skilled at feeling the 'bad' feelings very strongly. It also means that even if we do stumble across a good experience, anticipation or memory, we are geniuses at making them seem weak, bleached out, as though they happened to someone else. As a result, we successfully destroy most of the positive feelings from any potentially useful or supportive memory. This is vital to do otherwise the positive memories will spoil our 'well-crafted' low self-esteem irreparably.

In and out for low self-esteem

In this ELF, we need to remember to step into feelings of wrongness, worthlessness and incompetence; and make sure we avoid high self-esteem by stepping away from any good feelings of powerfulness, self-acceptance or success. This is summarized in the table for quick reference:

Pattern	Step into	Step away from
Low self-esteem	Wrongness	Acceptance, feeling okay, power, responsibility, abilities, and success

Exercise: ELF Check

Do you sometimes find yourself devaluing or distancing yourself from positive memories and experiences and immersing yourself in disempowering or negative memories or anticipations?

Yes/No

When you dû that does it get you a life you love?

Yes/No

Failing at the ELF

Once again, we can see the fragility of the ELF. It's easy to see that if we just switch this around so we immerse ourselves in positive life-affirming memories, anticipations or experiences and step away from the disempowering ones, then the whole ELF just falls apart, and instead we become a genius at having great self-esteem.

Step 4: Relationship to time

Each of the ELFs has a slightly different relationship to how we process time. You may not have considered this before but time is such an important part of our every thought and sentence. This is because to make any sense they all need to include a verb, which has a tense – a time reference – whether it's past, future, present, etc. We can see from the chart below the specific uses of time in the Low Self-esteem ELF:

Pattern	Past	Present	Future
Low self-esteem	Being wrong	Beating self up for past, present and future; and being wrong for still being wrong	Being even more wrong

Exercise: ELF check

Do you sometimes find yourself having these kinds of relationships to your past, present and future?

Yes/No

When you dû that does it get you a life you love?

Yes/No

Failing at the ELF

Again we can see that any change to how we choose to think of the past, present or future will completely change how successfully the ELF runs. For example, if you decide to predict a future where you are successful and confident or focus on your previous successes it will prevent the ELF from running.

Step 5: Internal negative soundtrack

First, everyone talks to themselves and it's not a sign of madness; it is completely normal. The only question is whether what you say to yourself is useful or destructive.

Each individual ELF has a mixture of phrases, some of which are common to many ELFs and some of which are very specific to that particular ELF. These are the best and most common ones for generating genius levels of low self-esteem:

- 'Oh heck!' (Or, possibly, something stronger.)
- 'Not again!'
- 'Why?'
- 'It's not fair!'
- 'I'm so bad!'
- 'I/it wasn't that good.'
- 'They would have done it better.'

It also really helps if you can also include any phrases that discount or marginalize any of your successes and especially those which compare you negatively to others.

Exercise: ELF check

Do you have a negative soundtrack that sometimes encourages low self-esteem?

Yes/No

When you dû that, does it get you a life you love?

Yes/No

Failing at the ELF

If low self-esteem is your ELF you probably recognize some of these examples. Comparing yourself negatively to others is one of the key behaviours and, interestingly, something people with high self-esteem simply don't do.

Imagine if you started to say the opposite things to yourself with the same conviction and authority that you currently use when telling yourself the negative things – just notice what would naturally happen as a result. If you start to *do* (consciously and intentionally) the things that people with high self-esteem dû without thinking, then the ELF couldn't work any more and you'd naturally start to feel the same about yourself as they do about themselves.

Step 6: Physiology

When I was a kid I was often told off at school for not sitting up properly but, being a rebellious sort of lad, I just ignored my teachers as much as I could, safe in the knowledge they had no idea what they were talking about.

It turns out I was wrong.

Later, as an osteopathic student, I studied anatomy and physiology, and discovered there are some sound reasons why posture is important. When we slump, we actually compress the ribcage, making breathing less effective. In turn, it's not as easy to get oxygen into the bloodstream, and this puts the whole body and especially the brain under a degree of stress. Slumping also puts stress on the upper part of the back (the thoracic spine). This is an extremely important area as a whole section of the nervous system (the sympathetic nervous system), which controls the basic maintenance, sewerage, plumbing and stress-response systems, leaves the safety of the spinal column and runs out through the body from this region. Slumping therefore compromises the effective management and function of all these vital systems.

In addition, there is an important arterial system called the 'vertebral artery', which carries oxygenated blood and fuel to the brain. It actually runs through a small tunnel in each of the vertebrae (bones) of the neck. As a result, poor neck posture can affect the flow of blood, oxygen and fuel to the brain.

There are many more reasons why posture is linked to physical function, and especially brain function, which I could bore you about for hours... but it turns out that not only is our posture incredibly important in terms of our spinal and physical health, it also massively affects our emotional wellbeing. Therefore, posture isn't just 'standing up straight', it means the whole way you carry yourself in any given moment. As a result, certain postures, ways of moving and gestures are very closely linked with certain ELFs.

To maintain this ELF it helps to increase inertia, reduce physical activity and adopt a low self-esteem posture – this classically involves:

- lowered head
- lack of eye contact
- shoulders stooped
- hands clasped nervously in front of body

Although there are many variations of this extreme caricatured version, just catch yourself when you're feeling/dûing low self-esteem; and notice whether your body posture is reflecting your internal thoughts.

Exercise: ELF check

Do you sometimes notice your posture encourages feelings of lack of confidence in certain situations?

Yes/No

When you dû that does it get you a life you love?

Yes/No

Failing at the ELF
I'm not a big fan of the phrase 'fake it 'til you make it', as this suggests you're still feeling bad inside and pretending that you feel okay on the outside to others. Instead, I would be much more interested in changing how you feel, or what you are dûing, to start with.

However, using your posture to assist you to get into a different state is a really useful asset. There's been some very interesting research[5] recently, which supports the idea that osteopaths, other physical therapists and some enlightened psychotherapists have had for years, that your body doesn't just carry your mind around, the body and mind are deeply interlinked.

Therefore being aware of your posture is central to your use of the tools in the 'integration' section of this book.

Step 7: Lacking a sense of control
When any one of the ELFs is at work, it really feels as if it's all just happening to us and there's little we can do about it. It's as if we have to just wait for it to pass, which puts us completely in the

passive, powerless, victimized position that we discussed in the section on 'dû' (*see page 53*).

It also leaves us with the sense that, since we can't sort it, we are reliant on others to fix it. We feel we must need someone else's support or an external remedy, such as friends, drugs or therapy, to cure or stop it. This is a problem, especially when we find those external supports either don't work or simply aren't always available when we need them – what do we do then?

With low self-esteem the fact that we can't even sort our lives out very successfully naturally further lowers self-confidence, which creates one of the many 'beautifully designed' destructive, self-perpetuating spirals that seem to populate so many areas of life where we get into trouble.

Failing at the ELF

As soon as we begin to recognize we do have some power, this piece of the Low Self-esteem ELF 'machinery' melts away because it thrives on, and needs you to have, a sense of powerlessness to keep you trapped in it. Once you've seized back the reins of control again, the ELF just can't function and it completely fails.

Having looked through this pattern, you should have noticed that when you dû low self-esteem you use these styles of thinking. And when you don't think in that way, you have high self-esteem and feel good about yourself.

Consider the bit of the recipe that you use most often – check out what would happen if, instead of dûing what you normally do, you started to do the opposite – what would happen to that low self-esteem then?

RECAP

So, you can see, from this detailed and 'upside-down genius' celebration of the skill of low self-esteem, that it's quite an achievement; much work has been put into reaching such professional levels of low self-esteem. So, if you've achieved excellence in this ELF at any point in your life then – well done!

We can now also see there are so many weak points in the Low Self-esteem ELF's make-up that render it very vulnerable to change. Altering any one of these steps will result in the whole thing crashing down.

Now you know that an ELF has a structure, you can see that rather than being a victim of it, unwittingly you are the engineer and caretaker of this amazing piece of machinery. And once you realize that, you know from now on it's going to be yours to command; just think of what you'll be able to do when you harness this amazing talent, this exquisitely designed machine, to something much more life-enhancing…

CHAPTER 10

Lesson 8: Spirals and Vicious Cycles

Looking at the ELFs (Excellences of Limited Function) gives a glimpse into the inner workings of the machine that has done such a brilliant job of creating trouble in your life. Now we are going to look at how these ELFs interact with your body and health.

Once again, as this is not the main focus of this book, this will be a relatively brief exploration of the subject. For a much more in-depth analysis of the link between the mind, brain and body you might find it helpful to refer to *Introduction to the Lightning Process*.

You may have noticed one of the key features of ELFs is their ability to self-perpetuate and generate problems, no matter how good or bad a situation. So, for example, if you 'run' the Stress ELF pattern, then in times of stress you'll be stressed and in times of calmness you could also stress yourself in a number of ways. For example, you could worry about forthcoming stress you're anticipating or, possibly, you may be nervous about the strangeness of feeling calm.

Linked to this is the idea of spirals and vicious circles, and an example of this would be anyone who is unfortunate enough to have (dû) panic attacks, which usually happen something like this:

One day, relatively out of the blue, they suddenly experience some very profound and concerning symptoms. The symptoms are, more often than not, purely a result of a large amount of the stress hormones (adrenaline, noradrenaline, cortisol and others) being pumped into the bloodstream as the natural response to what appears to be a 'threat'. Classic examples of these types of symptoms include:

- Fast-beating heart
- Quickened breathing or hyperventilation
- Dizzy feelings
- Nausea, stomach cramps and an urge to rush to the bathroom
- Sweating, hot and cold
- Trembling and tremors
- Racing thoughts

Unfortunately, as soon as they're hit with these symptoms, which are often very strong and overpowering, they quite naturally become more stressed.

Now we have the problematic situation where the stress of the original event causes the release of hormones and the production of the symptoms above, which in turn create more stress, more stress hormones, more symptoms, and round it goes.

You can recognize those kinds of self-perpetuating spirals in the thinking styles in each of the ELFs; and they, in turn, produce powerful physiological changes, many of which are driven by the 'flight or fight' or the 'physical emergency response'.

This response to threats and stress is well documented and designed to help us get out of emergency situations. The hormones produced actually make muscles temporarily stronger, faster and more powerful. It is thought that this physical response was set in place way back in human history when our primitive ancestors faced daily threats and challenges that were predominantly physical, such as dealing with wild beasts.

The problem is that activating these powerful hormones doesn't just affect the muscles; it also affects most of the body's systems.

COSTS

In fact, most, if not all, of the cells within the body, including the brain cells, are affected by this 'stress' response. Activating the muscles consumes large amounts of body sugar, and as the brain itself is the other great user of the body's sugar stores, when we switch on the 'stress' response our sugar supplies now have to be shared between two voracious appetites.

Changes in delivery of sugar, hormones and other essential supplies to the brain cells affect their ability to function – so stimulating this 'costly' system has a downside to it.

The body has limited resources and in order to 'fund' the switching on of these very powerful hormone systems other body systems have to switch off to some extent to balance the books. This is okay, temporarily, as normally our 'ancestor versus the wild beast' contest would be fairly short-lived, with one beating the other fairly quickly, and when you see the list of what's sacrificed to fuel the 'stress' response, you can see why it's not a system that was designed to be, or should be, constantly stimulated.

The body chooses to deactivate the systems least useful in 'threat' situations, which include the digestive, the sleep management, the healing immune and, rather importantly, our 'complex thinking' systems.

When these 'complex thinking' systems are switched off, due to being faced with a threat, we launch into a much more primitive way of problem-solving. The brain doesn't want to overload itself by having to process too many options, which may slow down its response time to the threat, and so limits itself to some very simple choices, such as run, freeze or fight.

Unfortunately, when you're stuck emotionally this more primitive system starts to work against you. Trying to work out how to be happy and fulfilled when using this primitive way of problem-solving just isn't going to work very well. We obviously need some rather more creative and thoughtful ways of approaching the complexity of life, rather than just limiting ourselves to:

STRESS SWITCHES OFF 'COMPLEX THINKING' SYSTEMS, AND ENCOURAGES MORE PRIMITIVE, EMOTIONAL THINKING – BUT THIS OFTEN MAKES THINGS WORSE.

- **Run:** This could include running away from the problem or situation – leaving a job or relationship instead of finding ways to work the issues out. Or it could involve mentally running away from something by ignoring it or focusing fully on something else like drinking or eating to excess so that we don't have to look at it.

- **Freeze:** Just pretending the issue doesn't even exist. Feeling trapped, stuck or paralysed and so powerless to do anything about it.

- **Fight**: This could result in being physically, mentally or emotionally angry or aggressive as a response to the situation, although dialogue and creative problem-solving could more usefully resolve it.

So running these ELF patterns not only makes us view the world and ourselves differently, it also messes with our brain and body chemistry. The hormone soup that the ELFs produce will directly make us feel 'out of sorts' by its influence on the body and the brain's functioning, and it will also prevent us from being able to think clearly and find our way out of 'bad' states and moods.

This combination of 'feeling bad' and our physiological inability to think about our problems creatively makes finding good solutions very tricky. And so we gather further experience and evidence of how bad the world is or we are, and the ELF's destructive cycle sweeps us deeper into a sense of reality where change is not only hard, it can seem impossible.

GOOD NEWS

But remember, there's good news. In the ELF chapters, we noticed how fragile the ELF's grip is on convincing us that the world is really that way. We also discovered that making only a small change to the recipe would release us from its power, and once again the brain works both ways for us; as soon as we start to break that destructive spiral it can't run any more. Instead we start to run a constructive spiral, where a change occurs that makes our brain work better, and the improved state makes us feel better, switching off those 'stress' chemical and upwards we go!

We're going to look at how we put that change into action, by combining all the lessons in this book so far in a dynamic and practical way. And, because we're already geniuses – great at consistently reproducing results, on demand, then it's bound to be easy to put these ideas into practice and get the life you love, NOW.

PART II
Integration

Any time you are not in the Present, then you cannot be living the life you love.

This section takes all the concepts covered so far and details the precise steps you need to integrate them into your life.

I've designed these steps to be quite simple and easy to follow, so you can put them into practice immediately. As we cover them, you'll see that behind the simple steps there is quite a lot going on. It's much like launching a space mission – it only takes the pressing of one button to launch, yet there's an immense amount of preparation, detailed science and behind-the-scenes work that's actually making the rocket lift off.

I'd recommend working through each chapter, taking your time to understand what is required and then using the exercises to put the steps together, so you become a genius at them too!

CHAPTER 1

Lesson 9: Making the Magic Happen

Having lived within the wild 'bad lands' of the ELFs for some time, it is going to be a relief to have a new map of some exciting territory to take you into the life you love NOW.

HAPPINESS AND FULFILMENT WORLD MAP

There are only seven locations, or 'positions', on this world map, which lead to happiness and fulfilment. I'll introduce them one at a time, in some detail. We will spend time exploring the purpose of each of them and what you need to do in each position. Once we've got familiar with each one, we will then look at how they fit together and start to put them into action. Go to www.lifeyoulovenow.com and sign in to get a handy colour version of this 'Coaching map'.

THE PIT

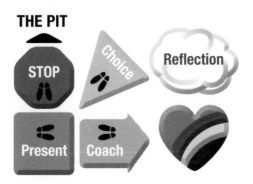

CHAPTER 2

Lesson 10: The Present

The square of being Present is our first stopping point in this new world. It explains the simple, but incredibly life-changing, idea of being in the Present moment; and this is probably the most important thing we can do. Being Present means various things to various people and is common to many philosophical approaches, but can be summed up as:

- Being aware of this moment.

- And aware that this moment is separate and unconnected to the past or the future – it just is.

- Recognizing that, right now, there is 'this moment' and nothing else.

Now although this sounds quite philosophical there is a much simpler and more practical truth to it, as we can spend a lot of time planning for the future, but very often the future doesn't work out in the way we expected.

As I'm writing in 2013, we've just had both the Mayan prediction of the end of the world (didn't happen) and a potentially close brush with a huge Earth-destroying asteroid 2012 DA14 (didn't happen either).

However, if either of these apocalyptic events had occurred, or to use a more feasible possibility e.g. being knocked down by a bus or car, then how important would next month's sales meeting/exam/date/court case/operation be? And how important would the 'now' that we have be?

Clearly the answer is that next month's events are irrelevant and the 'now' becomes intensely and immeasurably important.

And this seems to be the problem with humans and the Present; we are so rarely 'in' it. Instead, we are constantly thinking about other things: what might happen next, where we'd rather be, what we'd rather have, judging if something is good or bad, right or wrong and so on. In fact, the ELFs (Excellences of Limited Function) are totally about not being Present to what 'is' and instead being in some other version of reality.

And yet the Present is all there is...

Exercise: Being Present

Write down your answers to the following questions.

- How often am I Present to the wonder of the world?
- To the wonder of being alive?
- To the sun, trees, seasons?

There are moments when we are in touch with the Present, for example being in love, having a newborn baby, when we, or a loved one, have recovered from a serious illness, or escaped from a crisis or accident.

If you've experienced those kinds of extraordinary moments, you may have had the sense that you couldn't quite work out how other people seemed to be beavering away as normal. Somehow they were still getting wrapped up in the mundane daily stuff of life, unaware of the importance of the events unfolding in your life.

It's also funny how quite a few of these examples of being Present are as a result of escaping from dreadful situations. It's almost as though these moments are a wake-up call to make us remember what's really important.

BEING IN THE **PRESENT MOMENT** IS PROBABLY THE **MOST IMPORTANT THING** WE CAN DO.

Exercise: Recognizing the Present

Write down your answers to the following questions.

- Where were/are you most Present?
- How does it feel to reconnect with those experiences?
- How does it put the rest of life into perspective?
- What percentage of the time are you Present to the wonder of each moment? 0–10, 10–20, 20–30, 30–40, 40–50, 50–60, 60–70, 70–80, 80–90, 90–100
- Would you like that to be more?

And so, the hard lesson seems to be that, although we instinctively know that being Present is an essential part of gaining fulfilment, happiness and satisfaction, we seem to have an almost perpetual amnesia for this truth. I'd like to suggest the idea that:

Any time you are not in the Present, then you cannot be living the life you love.

The true purpose of this book, the steps of the process you're about to uncover, and according to many sages the true purpose of life itself, is to live a life where you are truly Present. And this is why the word NOW is given such prominence in the book's title.

Just take a moment to imagine what that might be like to be truly Present. When each day is a continuous stream of being in each and every moment as fully as possible, and relishing how it is to be alive in this moment; when we are aware and alert to the possibility and potential of each moment.

When I've helped people use the steps in this book to change their lives it's intriguing to hear what they report as being the most significant change. Although they have achieved their goals of deeper calmness, increased confidence and so on, one of the commonest things they say is that they noticed they were really

Present; they noticed the little things – the way the light was that day, the way the leaves moved on the trees in the breeze, the sounds of the city – and with that there was a deep contentment.

So being Present, or heading back towards that state when you're feeling a bit lost, is the compass heading for the rest of the book, and I'd recommend it, if you want happiness and fulfilment for the rest of your life.

And it follows that any time that you're not in the Present you're being distracted from what is really essential for happiness. And this takes us to our next stop on the map, the Pit.

CHAPTER 3
Lesson 11: The Pit

Welcome to the Pit. Although it's on the map, it's somewhere we aren't going to be visiting too often, as it really belongs on your old map of the world.

It's very important to recognize and fairly easy to describe, as it is *anytime* when you are not Present or anytime when you are not engaging in 'life you love'-enhancing activities or thoughts. I've found it helps to think of this in black-and-white terms: you are either having a life you love or you are in the Pit.

Being in the Pit is not a nice place to be, although if you are in it much of the time it may appear comfortably familiar.

The Pit certainly has degrees of unpleasantness. You can be paddling in its shallows or drowning in its deepest waters, but wherever you are in that dark ocean, you are still in the Pit and NOT in a life you love.

The only other thing to work out is whether you're treading water and at the mercy of its currents, swimming out deep into it, or heading back to shores of happiness. Identifying it is quite easy by asking yourself:

Am I having a life I love or not?

There are certain symptoms that will show you when you are in the Pit. These include:

- Losing your sense of humour.

- Becoming overemotional or losing a rational perspective.

- Feeling overwhelmed.

- Taking life too seriously.

- A lack of joy, happiness or fulfilment.

- Any of the ELFs (Excellences of Limited Function).

- Feeling (dûing) crabby/irritated/hopeless/jealous and any of the other states listed (*see page xii*).

- Being passive to something when you could be active (*see page 51*).

There are many other symptoms, but this list should make you aware of the main ones to watch out for. Use the following exercise to get even clearer about how much the Pit is occupying your life.

Exercise: Knowing the enemy

Ask yourself the following questions and write down your answers.

1. What percentage of the time am I in the Pit? (In my experience of asking this simple but important question I've often found that people will give themselves a more favourable percentage than they really should.)

2. To check this for yourself, now answer the question: How much of my life would I describe as really living the life I love?' And, by that, I don't mean an average okay life but a great life.

If your answer to the first question is, 'I am in the Pit 30 per cent of the time,' but your answer to question two is 'I am living the life I love only 20 per cent of the time,' then, in fact, you are in the Pit, to one degree or another, 80 per cent of the time.

Any trips into the Pit, short or extensive, minor or major, are going to cost you enormously, due to that important process we mentioned earlier, neuroplasticity (*see page 23*).

You'll recall neuroplasticity is the brain's ability to rewire itself as a result of how it's used. Pathways that get a lot of 'traffic' become faster and have a greater influence on all our brain function and types of thinking.

This is the danger of spending a lot of our brainpower 'training up' the neurology that leads us into the Pit. The brain works on the basis that if we're using a particular pathway a lot then it will use the power of neuroplasticity to make it easier to activate that pathway. The brain is just trying to be helpful, responding to the way we've been using it.

The downside of this helpfulness is that it means that accessing the Pit becomes even easier the more time we spend in it. As a result, the Pit pathway receives 'favoured' status within the brain. It becomes much like an 'A' list celebrity who gets invited to all the best parties, it gets to connect up to many different pathways, making it much more influential on all brain functions.

Additionally, due to the highly developed interconnectivity that comes with being a well-used pathway, thoughts previously unconnected with the Pit can now trigger it.

You'll recognize this aspect of our brain function in the following story.

The black VW Golf

Imagine I had a black VW Golf and it was my pride and joy. I kissed it goodnight every night, and polished it to a shine every Saturday.

Imagine my horror to find one day that my prized possession had been stolen, and when it was finally returned to me, it was a burnt-out shell.

Now, if I had read this book I would be able to deal with this better, but let us imagine for the moment that I had none of the skills of this book.

The next day I needed to go to town and I had to walk because now I had no car: can you guess which cars I noticed as I walked?

Yes, Golfs, and whether they were black or another colour, all reminded me of my precious black Golf and my loss.

Equally, if I saw the VW insignia on a camper van, guess what that reminded me of too?

In fact, all cars now reminded me of my loss.

When I saw other people walking, I noticed they didn't have a car either and this in turn reminded me of my car, and my loss.

On my way home I passed a park. As I gazed across the grass, I noticed some young boys having fun playing around.

I looked closer: and, yes, they were playing golf.

This naturally reminded me of my Golf again and my loss.

And that's how the brain works; it looks for patterns and connections, working hard to interpret the world based on these highly used pathways. The problem is, the more we spend life in the Pit, the easier it becomes to get into it in a millisecond's notice. And then the Pit becomes our life.

Now if that all sounds rather bleak, then it's time to recall there is some great news about neuroplasticity. Neuroplasticity is non-judgmental – it simply doesn't care which pathways we're activating, or whether they are good or bad. It purely develops and grows the ones that are used the most.

So the solution for moving out of the Pit, forever, is exactly the same one we used to get into the Pit – neuroplasticity.

Only this time you'll be exercising the pathways that move you towards the life you love, while stopping using the pathways that take you into the Pit.

If that brain-changing process was so effective that it was able to get us that deep into the Pit, then as long as you point your brain in the right direction, it will naturally be just as smart, rapid and effective at getting you into a life you love.

So your first job has to be becoming very good at spotting the Pit. When you think about it, this has really been the focus of the

YOU'RE EITHER
HAVING A GREAT LIFE
OR YOU'RE **NOT** AND
YOU'RE **IN THE PIT.**

book up until this point. All the topics you've worked through in the previous chapters, e.g. understanding genius, upside-down genius and picking through the brilliantly designed ELFs, have given you a deep familiarity with the detailed anatomy of the Pit.

SPOTTING THE PIT IN ALL ITS FORMS

Although, as mentioned above, it is essential to spot the Pit in order to move towards a life you love, I've found it's very common to lack awareness of some of the ways we have of heading towards the Pit. Most people are usually quite good at spotting the most familiar and powerful versions of it, but less good at noticing the Pit in all its forms and varieties.

So, for example, we recognize when we're unhappy or angry or being a victim, yet less likely to notice when we're irritated due to, perhaps, waiting in line at the grocery checkout, being stuck in traffic or bored because there's nothing interesting on TV. However, these versions of the Pit are just as important to recognize and take action to avoid, and the reason for this once again lies in neuroscience.

Not too long ago, when computers were slower and had less memory to work with, it took a long time between asking the computer to print and for the printer to spit out the finished document. The main reason for this was that the computer didn't have enough processing power to create the document in the word-processing program (e.g. Word) and run the printing program at the same time.

With the advent of smarter, more capable machines, when we open a Word document and press print, the printer immediately starts printing it.

This is due to the extra 'brainpower' of today's computers; they have enough spare capacity to predict what's likely to happen next. So, when you open a Word document the computer knows there is a fairly good chance you might need to print the document and gets the printing software ready and fired up, in the background, just in case it's required.

The brain does a very similar thing. It notices patterns and realizes that certain emotional states, such as anger, guilt or upset, all tend to be linked, and when we dû one of these emotions then one of the other ones quite often follows.

Seeing this link, the brain then creates, using neuroplasticity again, fast connections between the different groups of nerve pathways responsible for these various emotions. As a result, when one of these emotions is triggered, just like the printing software, the nerve pathways of those other emotions are readied and fired up in preparation for use. Each time this happens it exercises those pathways, making them stronger and easier to trigger.

Therefore, this is the problem of not spotting all the varieties of the Pit. If we successfully stop anger, for example, but continue to fire up guilt or boredom, then actually in the background we're really invigorating the exact pathways (of anger) we want to avoid exercising.

The brain also recognizes that there are certain emotions and therefore nerve pathways that rarely fire together; e.g. it's rare to move quickly from anger to happiness. As a result, there are very few connections between these two very different states.

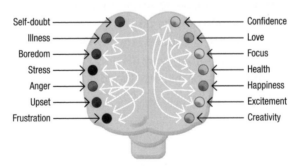

This is a symbolic image: the brain doesn't really have 'good' on the right side and 'bad' on the left side of the brain.

You can test this out by holding a pencil between your teeth while trying to think of something upsetting. You'll find it quite difficult to do because holding the pencil in this way raises your mouth into a smile, activating the nerve pathways of 'happy', which makes it less easy to trigger the pathways of 'upset'.

This ability to make connections between linked thoughts and emotions and the lack of linkage between unrelated areas is, again, good news. As you start to stimulate more happy pathways your brain starts to favour those new pathways. At the same time it also naturally becomes much more difficult for your brain to trigger the old negative pathways because there is such a poor connection between these 'happy' pathways and the 'Pit' ones.

THE NEXT STEP

Recognition that you are stimulating the kinds of neurology that lead you into the Pit is a brilliant lesson to have learned, and is a vital step in getting the life you love. However, on its own it only provides a theoretical understanding of the problem.

Much like an alcoholic's (or more precisely someone who dôes unhelpful choices around alcohol) recognition that they have a problem relationship with alcohol, it is very much the first point of change. However, just continuing to drink in spite of that recognition isn't going to lead to any meaningful improvement. To make real change, you have to move from recognition to action, but what action do you need to take?

Well, once you have become aware of when you are exercising your brain in that old 'wrong' way it's time to move onto the next waymarker on the map of the New World, the 'Stop'.

CHAPTER 4

Lesson 12: The Stop

You know now that nerve pathways grow and develop as a result of use, much in the same way as building muscle strength by exercising in a gym. Imagine if, for some reason or other, you went to the gym for six months but only exercised your left arm. After six months of weight training your left arm would be much more bulked up and stronger than your right one. If you then wanted to get your right arm stronger than your expertly trained left arm, what would you need to do?

It wouldn't just be a case of going to the gym and exercising your right and left arms equally, as your left arm is already much stronger. If you trained them equally you would just continue to emphasize the strength of that left arm and the right arm, although it would develop, would never catch up. Instead, if you want your right arm to become stronger than your left, you will need to just exercise that right arm and completely avoid exercising or developing the left one any more.

The nerve pathways are exactly the same. Our feelings, emotions, ways of thinking, experiences and behaviours are a result of consistent exercise of certain pathways to a genius level. This means it's important to recognize which pathways lead into the Pit, and then to no longer exercise them at all.

Once you've done that you'll need to exercise the good pathways, which I'll cover in the following chapters.

So the first action is to interrupt the neurological pathways to the Pit, and this is actually very simple to accomplish. All we need to discover is the power of the Stop.

So, over the next few pages you'll be going on a short journey into the world of the Stop. You'll learn why it's so useful and work through getting one that works really well, step by step. By the end of the chapter you'll have developed a deep understanding of the Stop and have an effective tool to make change.

HOW DOES THE STOP WORK?

It's very easy to interrupt those 'bad' neurological pathways because you already have an onboard mechanism to do this perfectly. All you need to do is access the neurology of what it is like to experience the feeling of a Stop and then connect that brilliantly effective piece of neurology to the pathways that have been taking you into the Pit. Once again, you can do this by using the power of neuroplasticity.

We already know that if you fire two neurological pathways at the same time, or one shortly after another, they will connect up with each other, and the more we do that the stronger the connections. Neuroplasticity experts use the phrase, 'nerves that fire together wire together' to describe this feature of the brain.

You'll see this phenomenon in the way the smell of suntan lotion might remind you of the beach, simply because the pathways of 'suntan lotion' and 'the beach' have been fired together a few times.

In the same way, firing the Stop pathways at the same time as the Pit pathways connects them up, and the Stop pathways obviously have the effect of stopping everything in its tracks.

How brilliant would it be to have those runaway pathways, which instantly catapult you into negative thinking and feelings, grind to a halt as though thick treacle had been poured into their workings?

So the next question is, how do we switch on the Stop pathways?

SWITCHING ON YOUR STOP

Well, it's not just a question of *saying* the word 'Stop'. Although that sometimes might work it is not usually powerful enough to interrupt these 'bad' pathways. Instead we need to fully access the pathways of Stop. Doing this will take a little time as you need to explore the key factors that will make this happen, the most important of which is 'congruency'.

Congruency

This is a key word of this book; you're going to read it, and think about it, quite a lot from now on. 'Congruency' means saying or doing something and ensuring that what you're saying and doing matches how you are doing it.

We are masters at spotting incongruity. A classic example is if, at the end of a date, someone says, 'I really like you, I've had a great time this evening, it's been really nice and interesting.' Although the words are fairly positive, you can hear in the way it's said that they're about to tell you they never want to see you again. This is also called the 'silent but', where everything they've said signals that they are going to deal you the knockout punch of why all the positive things they've just said count for nothing.

- 'I want to be with you, but...'
- 'We'd love to give you the job, but...'

It is also heard in phrases such as, 'I am not a racist/sexist, but...' Then you know that what is about to be said is either racist or sexist.

When we are being congruent we are 'really meaning it'. To do this, neurologically we are activating the main essential pathways, memories and diverse expressions of an experience.

When a politician or leader is being incongruent, it's really clear that they are not completely telling the truth or believing what they are saying. When we see a politician or a leader who is being completely congruent that is very clear too, we recognize it as being something they genuinely believe in.

YOU CAN ONLY GET
WHAT YOU TRULY WISH
FOR IF YOU ARE
WALKING YOUR TALK,
BEING CONGRUENT
AND AUTHENTIC.

So if you want to activate your Stop pathways effectively, it needs to be done in a completely congruent way so as to generate enough mental 'juice' through those pathways to make the Stop experience powerful enough that you can really feel it.

To create a congruent Stop you will need to re-trigger as many of the core elements as possible of that Stop experience. These elements will include:

- What you say – 'Stop'.

- The way you say it – your voice tone, volume and conviction.

- How you move your body as you say it, and so on.

DEVELOPING YOUR STOP

If you don't do the Stop congruently then it is unlikely to be effective, so I am going to guide you through the process of developing your Stop, step by step.

Step 1: Recall 'Stops'

Think about a time when you were very in touch with your Stop. Common examples include keeping a child safe by alerting them to some danger; they might have been reaching for a hot cup, or getting too close to something with some potential danger, like a dog or car.

Notice how it feels to say this kind of Stop. Check how you said it in your head and how it sounded aloud. What was your voice tone and volume? What were your gestures as you said it – and your posture, how was that? How were you standing when you said it?

Imagine you see a friend about to make a mistake, maybe they are about to cross the road and have not noticed a car coming towards them, or about to put diesel into a car that takes petrol. Again notice how it feels to say this kind of Stop.

Maybe you've had the experience of getting a call from a salesperson, trying to sell you something you already have or don't want, and you decide to stop them in their tracks, to avoid wasting everyone's time, and your Stop is so good they clearly get the message and leave you alone. Again, notice how it feels to use this kind of Stop.

Simply by recalling these Stop times you are firing up the part of your brain that knows all about Stop, and this will be very useful as you develop a really powerful easily accessible Stop, which you can use to change your life.

Step 2: The power of posture

I touched on the effects of posture on how our brains operate (*see page 95*). Now, we'll explore how posture affects our feelings even further.

And, as you're about to discover, it's going to be your secret weapon in the process of change.

We already recognize the link between emotions and posture: that posture can signal how we are feeling and, as a result, warn other people how they should respond to us. For example, you can often tell when your friend or partner is upset before they've even spoken about their problem just by the changed tone of their voice, or the way they walk towards you.

So as we recognize the clear link between posture and emotions, it may come as no surprise to discover that this is a two-way street: adopting certain postures will switch on certain emotional pathways in the brain, which in turn will cause you to have those feelings. We've already seen this with the 'pencil in your mouth' example (*see page 121*) – smiles are a 'posture'.

Posture is also very powerful as generally we adopt a posture without even thinking about it. As a result, posture is managed by the unconscious controlling systems of our nervous system. This is the part of us that remembers to breathe when we sleep, wakes us just a few seconds before the alarm clock does, raises our heart rate when we climb upstairs, and manages anything that works without us even having to consciously activate it. This makes it a very powerful force to have on our side. Let's look at the power of this unconscious ally with some exercises.

Exercise: Unconscious posture

Are you right- or left-thumbed?

Stretch your arms out wide to the sides. And now bring them together in front of you and interlace your fingers. Look down and notice whether your left or right thumb is on top.

Now repeat this exercise and you'll notice something very interesting.

Each time you interlace your fingers, you do it in exactly the same way.

Now try again, this time attempting to interlace your fingers the other way so that your other thumb is now on top.

The chances are you will find this really strange and it will feel odd and wrong. You probably didn't know that you have a preference for the way you interlaced your fingers, but we all do.

Why is this? Well, when you learned to interlace your fingers as a child, your brain decided to shortcut the process. It couldn't be bothered to waste time on choosing which way to interlace your fingers each time and so, at some point, made a decision to do it one way; and, ever since then, your brain's saved computing energy by doing it this way. This is a great example of neuroplasticity and the way our brain passes the more familiar, boring and repetitive processing to our unconscious brain.

Now try this second exercise.

In Western culture, nodding is connected to saying 'yes', so do this now and notice how it feels correct and normal. And 'no' is connected to shaking your head from side to side.

Now nod and say 'no' and shake your head and say 'yes'. Notice how this feels. It's so against what we've been trained to do that, for most people, it just feels wrong.

These exercises show how posture works at an unconscious level; and you'll be using the unconscious power of your posture to create a brilliantly effective Stop. But, before we do, there is one more thing to explore about posture.

Exercise: Mind or body?

To do this exercise, you will need to stand up and have enough space to move your arms around freely.

Posture one

As you stand, put your feet together, bend your knees, drop your head down and place your hands between your knees.

Notice how you feel standing this way. Most people say they feel small, vulnerable, put upon or a victim. A few people feel safe and empowered. It doesn't really matter which category you fit into, simply notice how you feel in this posture.

Posture two

Now, take on the opposite posture.

Stand up straight, with your feet wide apart, your head held high, arms outstretched and gaze upwards.

Again, notice how you feel when you are in this posture. Most people say they feel lighter, more empowered, happier or energized. Again, there are others who, instead, feel vulnerable and exposed or uncomfortable. It doesn't matter which group you fall into, just simply notice how you feel in this posture.

Testing congruence

Now, take on 'posture one' again and say the opposite to how you actually feel. So, if you felt small and vulnerable say, 'I feel big, strong and empowered.' If you felt comfortable and safe in this posture then say, 'I feel uncomfortable and uneasy.'

Notice how you feel when you hold this posture and say this 'opposite' phrase. Most people feel much as they did before – the incongruent voice doesn't really make much difference; it's not very believable.

Move now into 'posture two' and, once again, say the opposite to how you actually feel. So, if you felt empowered and energized say, 'I feel weak and vulnerable and tired.' If you felt vulnerable and exposed say, 'I feel completely safe and comfortable.'

Notice how you feel when you hold this posture and say this 'opposite' phrase. Again, most people feel much as they did before – the incongruent voice doesn't seem to make much difference.

In this exercise, there is a mismatch between what we're saying and what our posture tells us about how we're feeling. Rather intriguingly, the brain listens to what our posture tells us in preference to the self-talk.

This is due to our having been taught, somewhere along the line, that the self-talk in our head is the most powerful factor in determining how we feel. But, as we've just demonstrated, that is not the case. In fact, it's our posture that leads the brain to choose how we feel.

FMRI brain-scanning research at the Technical University of Munich[6] supports these ideas too. Researchers asked the participants to mimic angry faces while undergoing brain scans. The researchers were looking for signs of emotions ('activation of emotional processing') in their two patient groups, a control group (normal subjects) and a group who had been injected with Botox, and found some interesting data.

The Botox prevented the participants from making very angry faces or frowns, due to the paralysing nature of the toxin in the injection. This group had much lower activity in the emotional processing areas, (less active 'anger' areas in the brain) compared to those who had not received Botox. The paralysis of their face meant the movements their body was making just weren't congruent with 'anger' and so it prevented the switching-on of the 'angry' part of their brain.

So, we are going to use the incredibly valuable factor of posture in determining how we feel, to generate a really powerful Stop.

Step 3: The four Stops

In my research, I discovered that there are four very powerful postures and movements that activate the experience of Stop.

In each of the four examples following, the combination of using the word 'Stop' with a particular posture and movement very precisely activates the neurological pathways of Stop. What you need to do now is to run through each example in turn and notice which one creates the strongest Stop feeling for you.

Martial Arts Stop

1. Stand with your feet a shoulder-width apart, and hold your hands crossed at the wrists in front of you, at chin level. Make sure your palms are facing away from your face.

2. Uncross your arms quickly so your hands move apart, and say out loud, very clearly and precisely, 'Stop'.

3. Stop your arms sharply when your fingertips are pointing directly upwards.

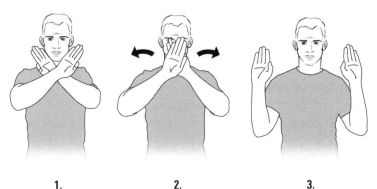

1.   **2.**   **3.**

The important thing to remember is to make this movement rapidly, like a martial arts move. It's also essential to avoid the movement ending by just fading out in a soft and floppy way; stop it precisely, cleanly and clearly.

Slash Stop

1. Stand with your feet a shoulder-width apart, and place one hand on the opposite shoulder – right hand on your left shoulder or left hand on your right shoulder, it is up to you.

2. Move the hand sharply and swiftly downwards across your body, keeping your fingers together, much like a karate chop.

3. Make sure the movement is rapid and precise, and say out loud, very clearly and precisely, 'Stop'.

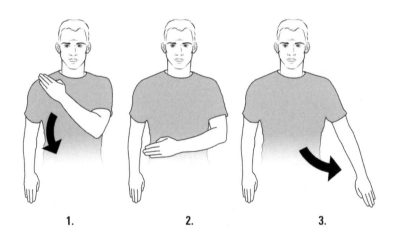

1.   **2.**   **3.**

Policeman Stop

1. Stand with your feet a shoulder-width apart. Bend your arms at the elbows and turn your palms so they face forwards.

2. Quickly extend your hands outwards towards the front, keeping your palms vertical, to make the classic policeman stop gesture. Once again, the movement must be rapid and precise. Make sure the end point of this movement is very clear, as though you have made contact with an invisible wall. As you do this say, very clearly and very precisely, 'Stop'.

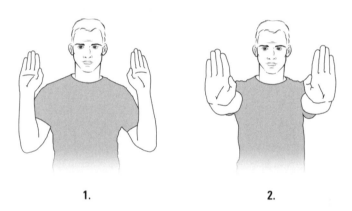

1.   **2.**

Buddhist Stop

1. Stand with your feet a shoulder-width apart, and place one hand on top of the other just in front of your belly button, palms facing downwards.

2. Gently and smoothly, push your hands downwards, letting them separate to each side as they go.

3. As you do this say, calmly and clearly, 'Stop'.

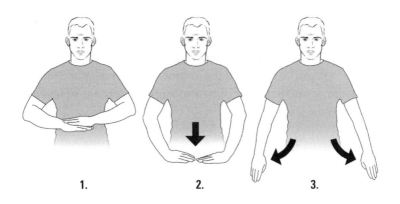

1.   **2.**   **3.**

Once you've practised these Stops a few times, choose the one with which you feel the strongest connection. As you go through the steps of the process, you may choose different versions of the Stop from the one that you've chosen today.

STOP ON THE MAP

Picture the first three positions laid out on the floor, or draw them out on a large piece of paper, as shown on the map below.

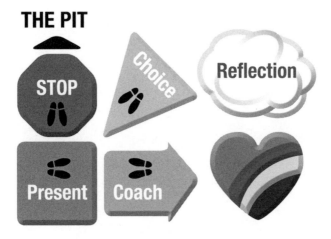

The happiness and fulfilment world map

Stand on the Stop location on the map, with your feet shoulders' width apart and practise doing your chosen Stop. This will be good preparation for the next chapter.

Now that you've unlocked the immense power of your Stop, it's time to put it into action at once and start the process of rewiring your brain for a life you love.

CHAPTER 5

Lesson 13: Running Through the First Steps

Now that you know how to use your Stop to reroute the very dominant and successful pathways that have been taking you into the Pit, you can start to exercise some new and much more exciting areas of your brain instead. What you've learned in previous chapters should also have provided you with all the component parts you need to make this happen:

- Knowledge of what is the Present.

- An awareness of the Pit in all its shapes and forms.

- A powerful experience of activating the neurology of Stop.

In this chapter, we'll work through how and when to use your Stop. As with most of these steps, once learned it becomes quite simple. However, let's start by looking at each element of the process and the steps in detail, so you really understand what you're doing and why. It may seem like a lot of information, but all the points are summarized in the next chapter so you'll have a handy guide to implementing the process as a whole.

BE CONGRUENT AND CONSISTENT

Congruence is vital to ensure that you're activating the maximum amount of positive neurology, as this will make the change become permanent. To help you to be congruent, begin by using these steps physically. In other words, stand up and walk around the steps in the very defined and specific ways that follow.

Although more rebellious people, and that would definitely include me, might baulk at having to do something by rote, this simple and structured approach is the most effective way of learning anything new.

When you think about it, it's exactly the kind of approach we use when learning to write or drive a car. When we learned to write, we endlessly practised getting the shapes of letters correct and when we initially learned to drive we kept our hands in the '10 to 2 clock face position' on the steering wheel, until it became automatic to do so. We didn't just mentally pretend to write letters or drive as a practise exercise, we needed to put pen to paper or get in the car to get the skills properly into our neuromuscular memory.

It's the same with these steps. Initially you'll need to do them physically and repeat them the same way each time, quite a few times until they become automatic. And just like practising writing an S, or a right turn in a car, you'll need to do each one with conviction, every time, as that's the quickest way to train the human brain.

However, in a few weeks' time, you'll have retrained your brain to head down into the new 'good' pathways and you'll be familiar with the steps, so can be more casual with your use of them. In the same way that now, when you jot down a shopping list in a hurry, you probably don't make every letter perfect but each is legible and, once we've passed our driving test, rarely hold the steering wheel in the prescribed manner, instead we do it in our own sweet way, knowing we can steer the car effectively in that way too. If our original training was effective enough, then if we ever have to write a really important letter, or find ourselves driving in dangerous conditions, or suddenly heading towards the Pit, that old original, reliable training is still available for us when we really need it.

So, the simple truth is that doing the steps differently from the way described below will just produce unpredictable results, but if you want fast, effective results then I'd recommend doing it exactly in the way that follows...

Start by picturing the first three positions laid out on the floor, or draw them out on some paper, just as shown on the map below.

THE PIT

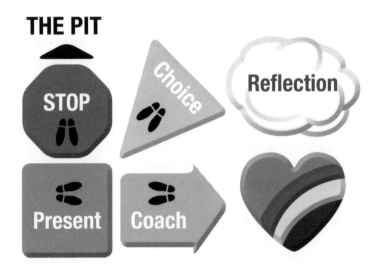

The happiness and fulfilment world map

Step 1: Start in the Present
Stand in the square of the Present; notice the footprints showing you where you need to stand and what direction you need to face.

Step 2: Spot the Pit
Begin by recognizing any one of the ways that you take yourself into the Pit. Let's use a common example of a 'Pit phrase':

- **'What if it**... all goes wrong and then the worst scenario imaginable unfolds leaving me feeling dreadful, fragile and stressed?'

Score

Very quickly score yourself out of 10, where 10 is feeling good and zero is not feeling good. Once you've done that, move to step three.

Step 3: Using the Stop

Now, you need to interrupt that neurology and those Pit thought processes, so use the Stop.

Placing the Stop

As soon as you notice the Pit, step from the Present out to the Stop position and insert your Stop, physically, just as you practised in the last chapter:

* 'Wh-**STOP**.'

And because you've interrupted it, the rest of the phrase after the 'Wh…' isn't said or thought.

Congratulations! Now you've learned the first three practical steps to getting the life you love, now.

STEPS 1–3 COMBINED

Let's just debrief what you've done and why.

Looking at the map we can see the Stop position is to the left of the Present with the footprints showing that you must step out to the left and also turn 90 degrees to look at the Present from the side. This means each time you're ready to use your Stop you need to step into this position and say your powerful Stop out loud, congruently, just as you practised in the last chapter.

Now if that seems like a lot to do, then you'd be right. The steps are specifically designed in this way. If we break it down we have:

* Recognition of the Pit.
* Identifying the 'Pit phrase'.
* Starting to say that 'Pit phrase' out loud.
* Interrupting it as soon as it starts.
* Stepping to the left.

- Rotating by 90 degrees.
- Taking up a very clear stance.
- Saying the word Stop, out loud and congruently
- Moving your arms and hands in a very particular way (the Stop actions) at the same time

That is a lot of steps and it takes most people a few times of repetition to get the hang of putting it all together, so don't worry if you start off being a little bit confused – just break down the steps a piece at a time until you feel familiar with it.

I like to make things very simple, so why is this process so deliberately complex? The answer lies in the computing power of the brain.

BRAINPOWER

Research in the 1950s by George Miller[7] into the limits of the brain's capacity for processing information, suggests that the brain is only capable of processing about seven pieces of information, consciously, at any one time.

We can visualize those seven pieces of information as occupying one of the seven available 'slots'.

1	2	3	4	5	6	7

If we fill the seven slots with Pit-inducing phrases then we will head into the Pit.

What if it all goes wrong?	It will cause the worst scenario imaginable	I am now imagining that unfolding	And thinking of how dreadful I'll feel	How fragile I'll feel	How stressed I'll be	How will I ever cope?

However, if, instead, we refill those seven slots with the steps outlined above, then there are no spaces left for the brain to think about the Pit at all.

Wh...?	Oh, that's a Pit phrase, isn't it?	I'm going to use a STOP	And step to the left	And rotate by 90 degrees	Stand in a particular way	Say, 'Stop'

So just by doing this, you'll have completely derailed the thoughts that were heading you towards the Pit and replaced them by a very clear, equally powerful Stop.

And that is the Stop element of the process.

On its own the Stop is very valuable at interrupting patterns and will give you a sense of relief, change and empowerment. However, this is just the beginning, because without further instruction the brain will just go back to its normal default pattern, which for many people will be straight back to the Pit.

This is actually why most techniques based on willpower alone fail; fighting the internal torrent of well-established Pit pathways is a long battle that is quite hard to win.

While on the subject of other approaches to change, you may have already recognized one of the problems with many 'just think positively' techniques. Although it's absolutely true that thinking positively is a great thing and the root of many modern approaches to a better future, unless you include some recognition and interruption of the Pit, it will tend only to be successful in a very limited way. Trying to be positive while undermining yourself by still being in the Pit is like putting a candle on a rotting fish and calling it a cake.

Before moving onto the next steps that will address how to avoid just simply collapsing back into the Pit there are a few useful tips to help you use the steps so far.

TRYING TO **BE POSITIVE** WHILE **UNDERMINING** YOURSELF BY STILL BEING **IN THE PIT** IS LIKE PUTTING A **CANDLE** ON A **ROTTING FISH** AND CALLING IT **A CAKE.**

TIPS FOR USING THE FIRST THREE STEPS

My experience is that when people first learn these basic steps it takes a little while to get the hang of them. They often also have some very common questions about these three steps that I've answered below.

Rehearsing

As this is a whole new skill set combining new ways of thinking, moving, acting and speaking make sure you give yourself some time to rehearse and learn the steps. Don't necessarily expect to master it on the first go, and remember to be kind to yourself, as this is an intrinsic part of this approach.

Spotting the Pit

This should be quite easy: remember you're either having a great life or you're not. There's also the checklist provided earlier to help you (*see page 116*), but another useful plan is to make a list of your 'catchphrases'.

I've found in the past that the term 'catchphrases' doesn't always translate into all cultures, so just to explain: a catchphrase is a very recognizable phrase, often used by comedians or chat-show hosts, which is so closely identified with their 'act' that it makes them instantly recognizable as soon as the first words of it are uttered.

So, in this context, a catchphrase is the very beginning of one of those phrases that takes you into the Pit. Becoming aware of them gives you a heads up, a red alert warning to the fact that you're heading towards the Pit. People often have many more than just one Pit catchphrase. Another good way to get familiar with catchphrases is to listen to other people's – you'll probably find that you know the catchphrases of some of your close friends, acquaintances and family members as these are warning signs to stay away from them, come to their aid, or get into an argument with them!

For some people, initially, they don't hear the catchphrase that took them into the Pit and that's fine, as sometimes it might be:

- A sound, such as a sigh or a grimace, a tensing of the forehead, etc.

- Or just 'feeling' down or in the Pit.

For some people, at least initially, the first time they are aware that they are heading towards the Pit is when they are deep in it and immersed in negative feelings. In this event they often aren't yet aware of the kind of thinking that took them into the Pit but we'll cover this in the 'Reflection' step later in the process (*see page 201*).

Whatever took you towards or into the Pit, whether you're familiar with it or not, the next step – the Stop – is always the same.

Placing the Stop

Take some of your catchphrases, or if you have noted down other people's catchphrases use them too, and practise working out where to put the Stop and getting used to saying the phrase and interrupting it with your Stop.

Choosing the Stop

If you find that the Stop is not effective at interrupting your Pit thoughts then it is invariably due to a lack of congruency in your delivery of it. If the Stop is not congruent it won't activate the powerful neurology required to counteract the very strong and robust pathways that take you into the Pit. When we covered the four different Stop postures you noticed that one of them appealed to you more than the others; having put the steps into practice you may find that you prefer a different one from the one you initially chose.

A general rule is to use a Stop that is opposite to the kind of Pit you are going into.

- If you're getting/dûing stressed and tense then very often a strong and vigorous Stop isn't what you need. Instead, you need a calm and peaceful one, as this is the opposite of the tense and stressed Pit, and the Buddhist Stop (*see page 134*) is likely to be the best choice here.

- If you're using the steps to relax and get to sleep at night then clearly, again, the Buddhist Stop is more likely to be useful than a shouting vigorous one, as you want to calm your nervous system down,

- If you're feeling/dûing a bit jaded or tired and wish to feel more energized then one of the more active Stops (*see pages 132–135*) is more appropriate. With time you will become an expert at choosing which Stop to apply for each situation.

Exercise: Using the steps

In a seminar, delivering this training, the trainer would spend a lot of time coaching you to use the steps. Using this book means you'll have to take that role, and the following exercises will help you to focus on the most important areas to work on.

Rehearsing

Open your diary and allocate a 10-minute appointment with yourself every day for the next seven days to rehearse these steps.

Spotting the Pit

Make a list of the first few words of every catchphrase or physical gesture (e.g. sigh, grimace, etc.) used by yourself, or others, which leads into the Pit.

Placing the Stop

Practise saying the first word or syllable of each of these catchphrases or physical gestures and get used to interrupting them with your Stop.

Using the Stop

Practise your Stop in front of the mirror or a video camera. You might want to ask a friend to give you some feedback on how believable your Stop is to them. Rehearse your Stop until it's congruent, believable and familiar.

Varying your Stop

Get familiar with performing an energetic Stop and also a deeply calm one.

ACTION

From now on, every time you spot the Pit, get used to using these three steps to start to make change.

1. Present

2. Spot

3. Stop

My experience is that the more you use the Stop physically and out loud in the early stages the quicker your brain learns, just like learning to play the piano or driving a car. However, there are times when it's not appropriate to do the steps physically or out loud, while driving a car or in a business meeting for example. In these cases there are a number of options:

- Take yourself off somewhere private and use the process.

- Do it on your hand, holding your thumb each time you use the Stop.

- When you're in the Pit during a conversation you may have noticed that you're so wrapped up in your internal noise that you barely hear the other person speak. As a result, you might as well go inside and perform the steps of the process to get back to being Present. It only takes a few moments, and then you'll be able to hear the conversation properly.

- Do the Stop anyway... probably not in a business meeting or in the car, but people have certainly used it in a shopping mall or with their family present, having decided that getting a life they love is more important than what strangers or family might think. After all, strangers are unlikely to notice, as most people are simply not Present or aware of what's going on around them most of the time! But where you do it is your call.

This point in your training provides a natural place to break. Now you've got some core tools to start making change with, so make sure you spend some time becoming familiar with them.

In the next few chapters we're going to move onto the final steps of getting a life you love.

CHAPTER 6

Lesson 14: The Choice and the Coach

The next two locations on the map will move you much further from the familiar territory of the Pit and into new ways of thinking and a new future.

At this point, I'm only going to cover the Choice position quite briefly; it will have a larger role later in the book, when we look at how to get around blocks. However, just because we are only attending to it briefly here, that doesn't undermine its immense importance in the process. In fact change is all about recognizing that you have a Choice in all situations, and especially at those times when it seems as if there isn't any. You could consider that all the positions on the map are about choice – choosing to get a life you love by taking real action. For the moment, however, we'll focus on the Choice position as a transition point between using the Stop to avoid moving into the Pit and choosing to move towards being your own Coach.

THE CHOICE POSITION

Stand in the Choice position on the map, and again notice the footprints showing the direction you need to face. Now you are between the route into the Pit and the route to the Coach, which leads you to a life you love. Your job is to weigh up the direction in which you'd like to go.

Similarly to using physical action to make your Stop powerful, there's a particular set of actions that can help you get in touch with the feeling of Choice. In this case, you make the gesture of Choice by placing your upturned palms in front of you, one to the right and one to the left and, while looking at your right hand (on the same side as the Pit) saying out loud:

'That way?'

Then immediately look at your left hand (which is on the side of a life you love) saying:

'Or this way?'

The best choice should be abundantly clear, so this step might seem slightly irrelevant, as *of course* most people would choose A Life You Love over the Pit. However, it's here for two reasons:

- The Choice position and action underlines that you're making a commitment to change.

- It's useful when you're feeling a bit stuck (which we'll cover in more detail in later chapters).

Now you've reaffirmed what you want from life, it's time to move into the Coach position.

THE COACH POSITION

One of the main purposes of this process is to move your internal conversation from one where you drift in and out of the Pit to a much more life-enhancing conversation, which has a very clear structure and leads you towards a life you love. This is the conversation that you'll develop between you and an inner Coach.

And because many people don't have a brilliant inner Coach, the first step is to develop one. In fact, the closest most people get to being coached is telling themselves they are no good and should do better. This, however, is not Coaching.

Instead pause for a moment and consider what would it be like if you had the most amazing Coach in your life – available 24/7, ready at a moment's notice, providing brilliant insights based on a deep and experienced knowledge of you, your past, your brilliance, and the ways you trip yourself up.

If they were on your team, it would be easy to achieve happiness, success or fulfilment... and this is exactly what you'll be learning to do.

BECOMING A GREAT INNER COACH

I can't overemphasize how significant and important this role is going to be in getting a life you love, so let's spend a bit of time discovering what makes for a great inner Coach.

One of the ways to learn about becoming a Coach would be for me to give you a long list of coaching qualities to memorize, but this would be the least useful way of doing it. I have actually included such a list in the book, but I don't want you to go searching for it yet. This is because one of the best coaching qualities is to ask effective questions rather than simply provide answers. In fact, it's so vital that I've written a whole book just about the most important questions in the world – *The 10 Questions To Ask For Success*.

Questions or answers

Why might questions be better than answers? In my experience, there are many benefits to having a Coach ask you life-changing questions. These include:

- A question focuses you on the issue you need to resolve.

- It makes you think about and discover the solutions for yourself.

- As a result, you're much more likely to remember it and get a deeper, more real sense of how that answer would make a difference to you.

- You provide the answer, rather than it being a good guess from an expert, so it's more likely to fit your needs.

- Unlike answers, which are limited to being very specific solutions to specific problems, questions can be reused time and time again. As a result they can, if used appropriately, continue to stimulate solutions and change in any situation.

For example, if you ask the question, 'Can you tell me what I should take on my trip?' The answer might be 'swimwear, T-shirts, shorts and suntan lotion' – all useful items for a trip to the beach, but not the Arctic Circle.

But if, instead of supplying advice, your Coach asks you the question, 'How will you find out what you need?' you'll be able to work out what's needed for this and all your future trips, without having to check in with the Coach for advice every time.

So questions make you more independent, self-empowered and in charge of your choices. This not only naturally makes you feel better about yourself, but also means you don't need to rely on someone else for support, which is important as they may not always be available when you need them. But your inner Coach and the great questions you're about to learn will always be on hand to help.

Exercise: Who knows best?

Write down your answers to these important questions.

- Do you notice that you spend too much time asking others for help or advice?
- Although it's quite nice to have someone giving you the solutions, do you notice that it costs you in the long run?
- Does being reliant on other people to point you in the right direction really improve your chances of getting a life you love?
- Who is most likely to have the best idea as to what makes for a life you love? Someone else or you?

I would say it is definitely you!

It's true that you may not have all the answers or even make the right choices all the time. However, I would strongly argue that is a much better situation to be in than to have someone else guessing or thinking they know what's best for you. No one else should be making decisions and designing your life for you. You above all others are best placed to make those kinds of decisions about your future. Giving someone else that important, influential role in your life is a fast route to the Pit, as it then becomes easy to blame everyone else for your problems and for not having a life you love.

Exercise: What makes a good Coach?

So, in line with good coaching practice, write down your answers to find out what makes a great Coach.

1. Who do you know who was a great Coach for you? Note down their name.

2. Who do you know who was supposed to be a great Coach for you and was actually a very poor Coach? Note down their name.

3. Who have you been a great Coach for? Note down their name.

4. Write down what you consider to be the qualities, talents and skills that were displayed by the Coaches in questions one and three.

5. Now when you consider the Coach from question two, do you notice that they were lacking in most, if not all, of these qualities?

Look back through your answers to these five questions, and you'll have uncovered part of the blueprint essential for a great Coach.

Now turn to the glossary (*see page 298*) and look through the list of 'great Coaching qualities'. As you read through, you may find that it reminds you that the Coaches in questions one and three had some of these qualities, which you may have missed out initially; and you'll probably notice the Coach from question two had very few of these vitally important qualities.

We can see from this that Coaching is not an inbuilt talent, it's a set of behaviours – something we dû. So the question is:

What kind of a Coach are you for yourself?

For many people the answer will be 'not great', so let's explore how that happened and what you need to do to get back to being a great inspirational Coach.

It's worth considering, just for a moment, your parents as Coaches. This book doesn't focus very much on the past, instead choosing the uncreated future to be our playground; however, it is true that our past is one of the factors that can tend to predict our future if we're not mindful of it.

Your parents or main caregivers, having such a significant role in your childhood, naturally play an important role in how you feel about yourself and the world. As a result, we very often end up adopting elements of their thoughts and behaviours into our own current inner self-talk – sometimes that's great, and sometimes it's not so useful. The question then becomes, if you have adopted them as your inner Coach, were they actually any good at Coaching?

If not, it's questionable whether they are suitable as a role model for such an important job.

ENTRY REQUIREMENTS FOR PARENTHOOD

If you go to college, to study medicine for example, then you'll need to have passed appropriate pre-college exams, in the correct subjects and with adequate grades. If you apply for a place at medical school with two fairly irrelevant qualifications, such as knitting and pottery, then they are likely to suggest you're not an ideal candidate for their course. This seems a relatively reasonable selection procedure. Turning your attention back to parenthood, a very obvious truth becomes clear – there is often a mismatch of the 'entry requirements' and 'skills required' for parenting

Exercise: Parents

First, note down what you think are the entry requirements to parenthood. What one single thing do you need to have done to be a parent?

Well, to become a parent (if we just restrict ourselves to standard biological parents) all you need to do is to have sex.

Getting to have sex can depend on many factors, including being lucky, attractive or drunk enough to make it happen! It can, of course, be for much more wholesome reasons, but generally we can see that the singular entry requirement for parenthood – having sex – is far removed from the skill set actually required to raise children effectively and brilliantly.

Next, note down what you consider to be the core skills require for raising children. This is my list:

- Being kind, compassionate and loving
- Being there for someone else
- Being able to give constructive feedback effectively
- Knowing when to take no 'nonsense' from you

Interestingly, they are fairly similar to the core skills of Coaching.

This mismatch of the 'entry requirements of' and 'skills required for' parenting is a huge problem. A result of this biological quirk is that people who aren't very good at parenting are left to raise young, impressionable souls. And if their own parents were poor role models, the problem becomes amplified.

Although as children we think of our parents as 'PARENTS' they are very often just young 'kids' themselves who've been thrown into the role, with no previous experience, or a complete lack of the vital skills for the job. And these inexperienced people are doing their best, but with little guidance or insight they are often quite unaware of the long-term effects their parenting may have on their offspring.

Looking at this we can see that if our parents weren't always the perfect role models they should have been, we shouldn't think too ill of them or blame them or their parents in turn, for our current problems (although it may explain the origin of some of the poor quality self-talk that many of us have).

It highlights that we shouldn't give that self-talk we've imported from them too much attention, as it's simply the echoes of an out-dated experience running in our heads years after the events are long past, often long after we have forgiven them for it.

If you've been letting these out-dated sound tracks have any airtime or influence in your life, since it's clear that *you* are in charge of running them, then you can also change them. And with that important background information in mind about your current inner Coaching, we can move onto the core steps of creating a great inner Coach.

HOW TO COACH YOURSELF

I designed this process so that even with just a small amount of instruction you can start to be an incredible Coach to yourself, but as with the earlier steps, you'll need to follow the instructions fairly precisely while you are in this initial training period. Just to recap the process so far:

1. Present

2. Spotting the Pit

3. To the Stop

4. To the Choice

5. To the position of the Coach.

Notice again the direction of the footprints on the map in this position, which look towards the square of the Present. Now, imagine you are a Coach and you're looking at yourself, standing

SWAP THE **CONVERSATION** THAT LEADS YOU TO **THE PIT** TO ONE BETWEEN **YOU** AND YOUR **INNER COACH.**

over there in that square of the Present ready for your Coaching input. As with all these positions being congruent is vital.

When teaching this process, this is one of the areas that often need lots of extra coaching and feedback, so it's essential that you provide this for yourself. And you do this by checking in with yourself and making sure you are being congruent.

COACHING CONGRUENCE
So, in this case, a congruent Coach is one who is saying the right words (and there will be a very short script for you to follow to start with) and 'walking the talk'. Everything they say is backed up by those qualities of coaching on page 155. There's absolutely no room for:

- Sarcasm
- Cynicism
- Undermining
- Criticism
- Doubting
- Negativity
- Giving yourself a hard time.

None of these appear in the list of Coaching qualities, and if you employed a Coach like that in real life you would be right to fire them immediately!

PHYSICAL CONGRUENCE
When you watch a great Coach at work you might see them take on a number of guises. They could be calming someone down who is stressed, inspiring someone who is doubting themselves, being kind and compassionate to someone who needs nurturing or giving important feedback that needs to be heard. However, in each role that they take they will be completely congruent.

Think about when you have seen a Coach at work – and remember coaching is everywhere – you might envisage a mother settling a frightened child, a football Coach inspiring his squad or a driving instructor stopping their pupil from crashing the car. When you think about it, you'll already know that:

- If they're calming someone, their voice will be softer; their gestures will be smaller, more fluid and graceful.

- When inspiring someone, their voice will be louder and more energetic, and their gestures larger and more excitable.

- When giving clear feedback, their voice will be calm and firm, and their gestures will match that.

In the role of Coach you will need to do this, too – it may seem like a lot of work but it's actually quite easy, because we already operate in this way in many different areas of our lives and are also aware when people do this well or when they do it badly. You may not have been doing a great job of Coaching yourself recently, so just make sure you recognize when you're not using the Coaching qualities listed (*see page 153*) and follow through with your commitment to yourself and a great future by becoming an awesome Coach to yourself.

CHAPTER 7

Lesson 15: Acknowledgement – Coaching (Phase I)

As you stand in the position of Coach, looking at yourself standing in the Present, there are three phases of Coaching to learn – and the first phase is 'acknowledgement', which is all about how your inner Coach speaks to you (Coaching phases II and III follow in the following chapters).

THE WORDS OF THE INNER COACH

Imagine that you're talking to the 'you' standing in the square of the Present, and with absolute authenticity and physically congruence, say the following phrases:

- 'Well done! You're on track.'

- 'You are a powerful genius.'

- 'You can do anything you put your mind to.'

- 'I will be with you every single step of the way.'

- 'I love you and admire you.'

- 'You deserve great things.'

- 'Everything is going to be okay.'

These are very simple statements, but my experience is that many people find it quite hard to say these incredibly important things authentically to themselves. Learning to let go of the resistance to being kind to yourself is probably one of the most transformational things I've ever observed, and many people literally get their lives back by just allowing themselves to be nice to themselves. As you learn to be a good Coach to yourself, it might be helpful to keep in mind this quote from Virginia Satir: 'We need four hugs a day for survival. We need eight hugs a day for maintenance. We need 12 hugs a day for growth.'

There is a phrase I use a lot in this stage of the process, which is: 'if you treated your friends like you treat yourself, would you have any?' Many people have been taught to confuse these two ideas:

1. Being nice to themselves and acknowledging themselves.

2. Being arrogant, selfish or too self-important.

Yet these are not the same things at all. The first is a good thing that brings joy to them and people around them, while the second only focuses on them at the cost of others, and is generally not so good.

There is an interesting story from the Bible, which highlights the importance of the first idea, when Jesus is asked which is the most important of the Ten Commandments. He replies that two are the most important.

1. Love God above all others.

2. Love thy neighbour as thy self.

This second commandment is often taken as an instruction to be nice to people and care for others, which is, of course, a good thing. But we can also recognize that Jesus is probably not saying, 'be nasty to yourself so that you can be nasty to your neighbour.'

This idea is echoed in many spiritual teachings, with the most obvious example being the practice of loving kindness from Buddhism, which I came across years after designing these steps. This is a practice in which you develop the ability to give out love and kindness to all things, but the first step is to give it to yourself.

So, rather than seeing 'being nice to yourself' as a selfish thing to do, see it as the starting point to making the world a better place. There's a lack of congruency and authenticity in someone who hates themselves, and yet spends all their time trying to be nice to other people.

If 'being nice to yourself' has been an issue for you then it's time to allow yourself to start being nice to yourself, not only as a gift to yourself, but as a contribution to others and the world as a whole. When you start being nicer to yourself, to be more fulfilled and Present, you can be of much more value to others. When you do this, your energies will be focused in the same direction and that will make you a powerful force for authentic change in the world.

The purpose of each part of the acknowledgment

In this acknowledgement phase a number of core ideas are presented. It is useful to explain why we use them, so that as we say each one we fully mean it. This understanding will also allow you to develop your own words and phrases to express these ideas with time.

'Well done, you're on track.'

This reminds you that you've just made a very powerful step in re-routing your brain and the direction of your life. This needs to be acknowledged as a brilliant thing to have done; recognition that now you are heading in **exactly** the right direction.

'You are a powerful genius.'

This reminds us of the important ideas of genius and ELFs (Excellences of Limited Function, or upside-down genius) that show you how you are incredible, determined and really good at things.

'You can do anything you put your mind to.'

This phrase is core to Coaching as it reinforces the Coach's opinion that, of course, you can be successful. It builds on the idea that you are a genius and have developed this incredible ability to steer your brain into the Pit. If you can train your brain that well, you can train it in a new direction to achieve pretty much anything.

YOU CAN'T BE
TRULY KIND
TO OTHERS WHILE
NOT LIKING YOURSELF.

'I will be with you every single step of the way.'

It can sometimes feel daunting to make a change on your own, but with this statement the Coach reaffirms that you're not going to be on your own any more on this journey. You now know the Coach is going to be there, any time you need them.

'I love and admire you.'

This is the Coach stating how important, valued and lovable you are to them. This is the statement that, as discussed above, some people can find the most challenging to say to themselves. If this is true of you, then you need to say it more often to yourself.

After all, if you don't love yourself, how easy will it be to let anyone else's love in, and is it likely to help you get a life you love?

'You deserve great things.'

Many people don't feel deserving of good things in their lives. And so, in a very similar way to the preceding idea, if you don't feel you deserve good things, then what chance is there of good things actually happening, or of you being able to embrace them if they do? If you find this statement challenging than it's a clear sign you need to say this more often to yourself.

'Everything is going to be okay.'

This statement reminds you of the idea of being Present. All there is is 'NOW' and it's actually okay. Being Present will help you feel okay about yourself and the way of the world, and is an intrinsic step towards getting a life you love.

Once the Coach has said all these great things to you (and with time you can tailor these phrases, but in the initial training phase I recommend saying them all as I have written them), it's time to step back over to the square of the Present.

RETURNING TO THE PRESENT

As you may remember, I mentioned earlier that the point of this process is to swap from having a continual conversation between you and the Pit to having a conversation between you and your inner Coach.

So now that we have extracted ourselves from the Pit and have had the first part of the Coach's conversation, it's time to step into the Present, and hear the conversation from that position.

Re-score

Step into the Present and re-score yourself out of 10, where 10 is feeling good and zero is not feeling good. You should notice improvement in your score from when you were in the Pit.

If the Coach did a great job, and you're able to really take that in, then you're completely on track. You should know this is the case because you'll feel some sense of support and positivity. You'll also feel a sense of either starting to see the light or being bathed in its brilliance.

Tips

If your score didn't change then there are two things to check:

1. Did the Coach do a good job in acknowledging you, did they sound believable?

If you felt the Coach could have been much better, then step back into the Coach position and do the Coaching acknowledgement step with even more congruence.

2. Did you listen to your Coach saying those great things to you and **_actually_** take them in?

If you felt the Coach was good but you were just dûing 'unable to take it in', this is a good example of a non-life-enhancing behaviour, which means you're headed into the Pit – and every time you get into the Pit you need to make a Stop, and use the usual steps to get out.

Using this approach will ensure that your Coaching is brilliant and you're able to accept and take in the acknowledgement of your Coach.

ACTION

Now you've completed this section, every time you spot the Pit use the steps to become a brilliantly effective Coach, who will acknowledge how amazing you are, support and inspire you.

Once again, it's worth pausing your training here and practising what you've learned so far, as these simple first steps are incredibly powerful in nurturing yourself and rewiring your 'positive self-regard' to become your normal way of being.

The more time you spend exercising the pathways of success and happiness and the more you let the old negative pathways waste away through disuse, the more you'll have of a life you love.

When you're ready to continue, which can be immediately if you have the time, we'll move into phase II of Coaching.

CHAPTER 8

Lesson 16: The First Coaching Question (Phase II)

Start by stepping back into the Coach position (you'll be doing this movement a lot from now on), as you activate the new 'How do I get a life I love' conversation, which replaces the old one between you and the Pit.

In phase II of Coaching, the Coach always asks the same, very powerful and important question:

'What do you want?'

This seemingly simple question is so important as it provides the essence for designing a future based on the free choice of working out **what you want** right now in this moment.

For many people, asking and answering this question may have been quite difficult in the past, because the neural pathways created by being in the Pit makes it impossible to make clear decisions – as you now know, being in the Pit means focusing on problems rather than solutions.

Once you're free of the Pit, however, answering this question becomes very different. You start to realize the unlimited potential of this creative question, and see that it's so flexible that it can be applied to virtually any situation as each time it is still exactly the right and best question to ask.

Having asked this vital question, step back into the Present to discover your answer.

THE QUESTIONS AND ANSWERS 'SEQUENCE'

You'll quite quickly get used to these steps between the Coach and the Present. Notice that:

1. The Coach asks the question.

2. You return to the Present to answer.

This very clear sequence retrains your brain to become familiar with asking questions in one place and then answering in another. In a short time the Coach position becomes connected with being positive and asking questions and the Present becomes linked to being acknowledged and answering questions effectively. This consistency helps this process to run much more smoothly and become automatic much more quickly.

RULES FOR ANSWERING THE QUESTION 'WHAT DO YOU WANT?'

The real power of the 'What do you want?' question comes from making sure your answers head you into a great future and further away from the Pit.

To do this make sure your answer fits these three rules:

1. Use positives.

2. Is it deliverable by you? It doesn't involve anyone or anything else having to change.

3. Use big, dramatic, congruent language.

It's pretty simple really but the rest of this chapter will guide you through how to use these rules, which can be easy to break without noticing in the early stages.

RULE #1: USE POSITIVES

The first thing is to ensure that your answer is stated in 'positives', rather than what is called 'negative wants'. Once again the reason for this lies in the way our neurology works, as the next exercise demonstrates.

Exercise: Einstein exercise

For the next two seconds I would like you **not** to think about Albert Einstein riding a purple goat.

Notice what happened when I asked you to do that. I expect that you immediately thought about Albert Einstein riding a purple goat.

The brain can't process 'negatives', such as 'don't think', without first understanding the instruction. And to understand the instruction it has to process the idea of 'Einstein riding a purple goat' so it can be ready to 'not think' about it. As a result, an instruction with a negative always has completely the opposite effect than the one it was designed to get.

In the same way, you'll hear people say, 'I'm not at all negative, I spend all my time making sure I am not stressed.'

Highlight the words in this phrase that are negative wants – instructions to the brain that ask it **not** to do things.

You should have spotted 'not negative' and 'not stressed'.

Here, in this very simple statement, their language clearly shows up what's really going on inside their brain: a whole heap of negative processing. This kind of unintentional brain activity has been confirmed in recent brain imaging studies.[8]

What is intriguing is this type of language is completely at odds with what they actually thought they were being, in this case, 'positive'.

Spotting negative wants

These are covered in even more detail in *Dû – Unlock Your Full Potential With A Word*, but these tips will help you spot negative wants easily.

Nots

Be aware of anything that starts with a:

- Not
- No
- Un-
- De-

Examples of this are:

- 'I just want to feel not worried.'
- 'I just want to feel no stress.'
- 'I just want to feel unworried.'
- 'I just want to feel de-stressed.'

Something-free

Also watch out for anything that has the word 'free' in it:

- Pain-free
- Stress-free
- Worry-free
- Hassle-free

These immediately trigger the exact opposite pathways to the ones intended.

Hidden negatives

There's also a category of very sneaky words that are negative wants but sound brilliantly positive; statements referring to the negative state without mentioning it directly.

For example, saying 'I want to be *free*' sounds great but, in this case, it highlights wanting to be free *from* something. This draws your attention back into the Pit and what is making you feel *not* free, e.g. oppression, stress, etc., which throws us once again back into the Pit. Other examples include:

- Protected (from)
- Safe (from)
- Secure (from)

Super hero statements

I've called them this because they are the kind of tag line a super hero would have:

BOLD, BRAVE, STRONG, COURAGEOUS AND UNAFRAID OF DANGER!

- 'I want to be bold.'
- 'I want to be brave.'
- 'I want to feel strong.'
- 'I need to be courageous.'

If you have to feel any of these things, then you must be doing something that is quite scary and fearful, and so these sorts of statements take you back into the Pit. For example, if someone says, 'I'm going to be very brave and go swimming,' this tells us something about how they feel about swimming, and that swimming is something they fear in some way.

In control

Saying 'I want to be in control' of something, again, sounds great, but the things we need to 'control' are usually inherently chaotic, unpredictable, troublesome or dangerous. Notice where the word 'control' normally shows up in language:

- Drug control
- Traffic control
- Control of dangerous dogs
- Crowd control

- Weight control
- Bladder control

If someone came back from a trip overseas and you asked, 'How was it?' And they replied, 'It was full of control,' it doesn't sound too positive does it? To avoid this pitfall, it's usually best to replace the words 'in control' with 'making great choices'. So 'I want to be in control' becomes 'I want to make great choices'.

End of rule #1
Wow! 'What do you want?' is such a simple question yet, as you can see, there are so many ways that can have us spinning straight back into the Pit, without even knowing we were doing it.

However, now you have this deeper understanding of what you need to do to answer this question properly, you will find your life will change dramatically for the better.

So from now on if you hear yourself giving these types of 'negative' answers, simply step back into the Coach position then kindly and compassionately Coach yourself by saying, 'That's great AND can you turn that into a true positive please.' Notice we avoided using BUT and replaced it with AND because, as mentioned earlier (*see page 125*), anything preceded by the 'but' is undermined by it.

Once you've got your head around this rule it's quite easy to put into practice – just make sure you're being genuinely positive with your language.

RULE #2: IS IT DELIVERABLE?
There is a quick check you need to perform on each of the statements that you give in response to the 'What do you want?' question and that is, 'Is it deliverable by me?' So always ask: 'Am I the person who has the power to make this happen?'

For example, if your answer to 'What do you want? is 'I want to be calm,' then you *are* the person who can make calmness happen in your life, so it passes this test.

THE REAL **POWER** OF ASKING **'WHAT DO YOU WANT?'** IS MAKING SURE YOUR **ANSWER** HEADS YOU INTO A **GREAT FUTURE.**

However, if you answer 'I want my boss to be nicer to me,' then recognize this as being undeliverable because your desired outcome depends on 'I want **the other person or thing** to do something.' Although you may really want it, you clearly cannot *make* your boss do what *you* want them to do. In fact, as you've probably noticed in the past, you can't really make anybody change unless they want to. The only person you have real power to change is you. Trying to change *the other person* is like trying to control the weather.

Making your 'wants' deliverable
To turn this answer around and make it deliverable:

- Coach: 'How do you want to respond to **your boss [or other person or thing]**?'

- Answer, in this example: 'I want to be **relaxed and happy**, independent of what **my boss** does.'

Let's consider another example. You're stuck in traffic and answer the 'What do you want?' question with: 'I want the traffic to flow freely.' It's easy to realize that this is undeliverable, as you know you can't really change the traffic.

So the Coach asks: 'How do you want to respond to the traffic [or other person or thing]?'

The answer: 'I want to be calm and positive, independent of what the traffic does.'

Making sure your answer is deliverable by you puts you back in charge of how you feel about things, instead of being dependent on your boss's mood, the traffic, or how anyone or anything else is on any particular day.

By responding in this way, you become like the football player we discussed earlier (*see pages 68–70*) who delivers his best penalty kick absolutely independent of whether the team is winning or losing.

RULE #3: USE BIG, DRAMATIC, CONGRUENT LANGUAGE

The final rule in this section is all about using more of the sort of language that activates the kind of neurology that we want to be stimulating.

So, for example, 'I want to be calm' becomes 'I want to be profoundly calm' or 'deeply' or 'powerfully' or 'extremely' or 'very' or 'totally'.

This is important because the Pit is filled with this kind of big dramatic language too, for example: 'I feel so down, deep dark, intensely and painfully immersed in the weight of these horrific feelings.' And you know how successful the Pit has been at triggering you into feeling certain powerfully negative ways, so learn from this and make sure that your positive statements are equally big and dramatic too.

And of course, when giving these powerfully uplifting answers, make sure you match them with your movements, voice tone and body posture.

Saying, 'I want to be deeply happy' in a flat tone, with a slumped body, like Droopy, the totally down cartoon dog, or Eeyore the depressed donkey in A.A. Milne's *Winnie the Pooh* stories, will **never** work, as there's too much confusion in your brain for it to able to take any clear instructions from such a mixed message.

Equally, saying 'I want to be deeply relaxed' in a hyper, fast voice, like characters such as Speedy Gonzalez the cartoon mouse or the hyper-bouncy Tigger, while having an incredibly on-edge, high-alert posture will **never** work either.

Playfully allow yourself to generate some more exotic and exuberant language around what you want, as this is the way to ensure it will become part of your future.

'Like a...'

It can also be very helpful to come up with an image, symbol, metaphor or simile to describe what it is 'you want'. Doing this seems to activate another set of parallel neurological pathways, which deepens the connection between you and your goal – getting a life you love.

The easiest way to create this alternative pathway is to use the phrase, 'Like a...' So if your answer to the 'What do you want?' question is: 'I want to have a deep and profound sense of peace,' then your Coach would ask, 'Like a...?' This allows you to answer in any number of ways. You might say:

- 'Like Buddha.'
- 'Like a rock in a mountain stream.'
- 'Like a cat sunning itself on a summer's day with the light streaming in through a window.'
- Or you might choose someone you know: 'Like my friend Mary.'
- Or someone you think has those qualities: 'Like Nelson Mandela.'

It's best to avoid statements such as, 'Like I used to be,' as this reminds you that you're not that way any more and so has the potential of taking you into the Pit.

RECAP

If it seems like a lot to think about when answering one single question, then relax! With practice, this knowledge will become second nature and if you do go off track, then you'll have a useful reference of the steps required to get back again.

In the meantime, let's finish by applying the question we first met in the Pit chapter (*see page 115*): 'What if it all goes wrong and then the worst-case scenario imaginable unfolds leaving me feeling dreadful, fragile and stressed?' In response, move through these now familiar steps:

1. Present
2. Spot it – score out of 10
3. Stop

4. Coach – acknowledge

   » Present – re-score

   » Coach – 'What do you want?'

   » Present – 'To feel deeply calm and confident about my future, like an eagle soaring on the wind.'

Obviously, this will not necessary be your exact answer. There are an infinite number of great answers to this question and each one will be tailored by you and depend on what **you** want in that particular moment. So go ahead and start to enjoy using this new set of skills to move your brain into new territory and a new future.

Re-score

Once you've answered the question brilliantly, re-score yourself out of 10, where 10 is feeling good and zero is not feeling good. You should notice a significant improvement in your score.

ACTION

Now you've completed this section you should have an outstandingly effective answer to the question, 'What do you want?'

Once again, pause your training here and practise the steps you've learned so far. Now anytime you spot the Pit, you Stop, your Coach acknowledges you and you move through answering the first Coaching question.

Each time you do that, you will be rewiring your brain, firing up the creative enquiring pathways that build exciting ideas about what you want in your life.

Just doing this will start to make opportunities show up in your life, allow you to be more Present and experience the life you love.

When you're ready to continue we'll go on to phase III of the Coach position and discover the second Coaching question.

CHAPTER 9

Lesson 17: The Second Coaching Question (Phase III)

So far you've moved from the Pit, through your Stop and made a Choice to Coach yourself. The Coach has been very kind and acknowledged you as a genius. You've accepted that acknowledgement, and asked and answered the powerful question, 'What do you want?'

Now you know the answer to 'What do you want?' it's time to step back into the Coach position and ask the second Coaching question:

'And how you are going to do that?'

DELIVERY

Naturally the inspiring Coach asks this question from the point of view of 'And you can have anything you wish for – what would you love to have?' This question should ***never*** be asked, 'And how *on Earth* are **you** ever going to get that?'

Once asked, move back into the Present to discover the answer. There are two ways to answer this question:

1. By changing your state.

2. By making an action plan.

CHANGING YOUR STATE

We covered states, or states of mind, in an earlier chapter (*see page 56*) and very often the answer to 'and how are you going to do that?' is a state, such as being calm, happy, motivated or confident.

In this type of answer, which is probably the one you'll use most of the time, it's all about choosing to feel different instantly and so is probably one of the most important skills you'll ever learn. But to do this effectively you need to know a bit more about how the brain, and especially emotions and feelings, work.

One of the easiest ways to understand how the brain gets in touch with powerful experiences is by considering the example of two people approaching an interview, as the following story demonstrates.

The interview

These two people, let's call them Gordon and Brad, have both attended many interviews in the past and got a number of those jobs. However, Gordon feels he is very 'good' at interviews and Brad loathes and fears them, and considers himself 'bad' at interviews.

Now, imagine for a moment that the brain's memory banks are a little like sets of three-drawer filing cabinets: the top drawer marked 'good memories', the middle drawer 'average memories' and the bottom drawer 'bad memories'. It's easy to predict which memories Gordon or Brad accesses when they think about the forthcoming interview.

Memory recall

Gordon goes straight to the top drawer of good memories and reminds himself of all the times he's had successful interviews, when he was confident and communicated well with the interviewing panel.

Brad, however, goes straight to the bottom drawer of his memory filing cabinet and reminds himself of all his experiences of dreadful interviews.

What's interesting is that both Gordon and Brad have a mixture of good and bad interview experiences. Gordon didn't get every job he went for and Brad was successful in some of his interviews; however, Gordon doesn't spend any time looking in his bad memory drawer and Brad never looks into his good memory drawer.

Predictions

They also both predict what's likely to happen in the forthcoming interview. Gordon imagines the whole thing going fantastically well – they like him, ask him the right questions and he performs at his best. Brad, of course, imagines the whole thing going wrong; they don't like him, they ask tricky questions, he even gets easy questions wrong and makes himself look a fool.

Voice-over

Finally, they both talk to themselves, but the voice-over or soundtrack each one runs is quite different.

Gordon tells himself how great he is at interviews, how much they're bound to like him and how lucky they are to have him as a candidate. Brad tells himself how terrible he is at interviews, how they're bound to hate him on sight and how quickly they are going to want to end the interview, knowing he is an appallingly bad candidate for this job.

As a result of these ways of thinking Gordon will clearly be 'set up' for success and in a much more interview-ready state than Brad; their posture and appearance will be congruent with this – Gordon walking into the room confidently and Brad shuffling in like a cow to the abattoir.

The interview process will unfold with a relative inevitability: Gordon is very likely to be offered the job, while Brad is not.

Powerful movies

This story demonstrates an interesting phenomenon of the mind. In order to make a memory, or any prediction about the future, so emotionally strong that it affects you powerfully, you need to be

'IN' the movie of the memory or prediction. By 'IN' I mean seeing the events unfold in front of your eyes, as if it were really there.

The other option is to be 'OUT' of the movie of the memory or prediction, so any position or perspective other than your point of view. This could be seeing it from above, behind, from the interviewer's perspective, etc.

The reason the 'IN' perspective creates such strong feelings is that's how we go through the world, by looking out through our eyes. However, we can recall things from a different perspective but, as this won't produce as much neurological activation, it will have less powerful feelings attached.

You may recall this from the ELF (Excellence of Limited Function) chapter (*see page 29*) when, in order to feel bad feelings fully, we have to immerse ourselves in the negative memories and reduce the impact of positive memories by stepping out of them.

Exercise: Rollercoaster

Imagine being on a rollercoaster (don't do this exercise if you're very scared/phobic of rollercoasters).

Run a movie of a rollercoaster and put yourself 'IN' the position of being in the seat of a big scary rollercoaster. See the track disappear in front of you to be replaced by the yawning expanse of the open sky as you reach the top of the track.

If you do this from your own eye's point of view, you'll feel the powerful feelings of being on a rollercoaster. If you like rollercoasters it will feel exhilarating, if you don't like them it will be scary.

Now, imagine watching yourself on that rollercoaster – this is the 'OUT' perspective. As long as you stay distant from it, your feelings will dissipate and fade. (If you have a strong fear of rollercoasters there is a good chance you'll try and step back into the rollercoaster movie; if you do that you will continue to feel scared. So make sure you continue to remain watching it rather than being in the movie.).

From this example, you can see that:

Stepping IN to a movie increases it – steps it up.

Being OUT of it decreases it – fades it out.

In much the same way when you recall 'detailed' memories or predictions you'll feel more powerful emotions, while having much vaguer memories or predictions will result in vaguer, less emotional feelings.

So think again about the two interviewees, Gordon and Brad, and consider the following questions and answers:

Q: When Gordon reminds himself of a positive memory of an interview, which makes him feel powerfully confident, is he 'IN' that memory or 'OUT' of it?

A: He is 'IN' it because the emotions are powerful.

Q: Do you think the memory is detailed or vague?

A: It is 'detailed' because again the emotions are powerful.

Q: When you think about Brad, reminding himself of a negative memory of an interview – which makes him feel powerfully nervous – do you think he is 'IN' that memory or 'OUT' of it?

A: He is 'IN' it because the emotions of nervousness are powerfully strong. They are not good emotions, but they are powerful. It would be much better for him if he were 'OUT' of that memory, as being so deeply 'IN' it causes him to shake before interviews.

Q: And is he recalling it in a detailed or vague way?

A: Again you know he has recalled it in a very detailed way because he feels very powerfully strong emotions about it.

You might also recognize that Gordon and Brad do exactly the same with their predictions about the outcome of the interview; they feel strong emotions about it, so they are both IN a very detailed version of the movie. In addition, accompanying both Gordon and Brad's very different movies and predictions is an authoritative, convincing and strong voice-over.

So when we consider the difference between Gordon and Brad in an interview situation we can see something very intriguing. They both have the ability to recall specific memories from a wide selection of memory options. Both are able to immerse themselves 'IN' their memories to make them very emotionally powerful and recall these memories in great detail. They also do that with their predictions about the future too, and run an internal voice-over that is authoritative, convincing and strong. In fact the only difference between Gordon and Brad is which memory they choose to get out of their filing cabinet and what the content of that voice-over is.

In this way, it's easy to realize that the difference between people who are good at interviews (or speaking in public, going on dates, etc.) and those who are not – or more precisely, those who dû good interviews or dû poor interviews – is minimal. And to change from dûing bad interviews to good interviews is a very simple process of learning how to select better memories and voice-overs.

There is one even more intriguing result of this understanding.

Once we recognize that we're free to select which memories we use, this changes how we respond to our future – and this applies to every one of our behaviours, every single way of being and every single situation.

This means finally you can be powerful in any situation, independent of your past, of who you thought you were, or of what you were told were your limitations.

The keys to the kingdom are yours!

ANSWERING THE SECOND COACHING QUESTION: 'AND HOW ARE YOU GOING TO DO THAT?'

Using this knowledge you're now ready to create a brilliant life-changing answer to this question. For example:

- Start with the Pit question: 'What if it all goes wrong and then the worst scenario imaginable unfolds leaving me feeling dreadful, fragile and stressed?'

CHOOSING TO FEEL DIFFERENT INSTANTLY IS ONE OF THE MOST IMPORTANT SKILLS YOU'LL EVER LEARN.

- Stop

- Choice

- Coach asks first Coaching question: 'What do you want?'

- Answer (for example): 'To feel deeply calm and confident about my future, like an eagle soaring on the wind.'

- Step back into the Coach position and ask your second Coaching question: 'And how are you going to do that?'

Well, if Gordon was able to feel confident about interviews by recalling a time of being confident in interviews and Brad was able to feel deeply nervous by recalling a time of feeling deeply nervous in interviews, if you wish to feel deeply calm and confident, then all you need to do is go back into a memory of a time when you felt exactly that way. Simply take yourself back to a specific time now where you felt deeply calm and confident.

Let's say, for example, you choose to go back to sitting on the beach that you went to every morning when you were in Mexico in 2001.

To make it really detailed you would remember one particular morning. Let's imagine it was when you got up early and went down to the beach. Nobody else was there; you remember just sitting with your feet being washed by the beautiful clear blue water of the ocean waves.

This kind of level of detail is exactly what you need to boost the amount of activity in the nerve pathways connected to that moment. You might find some helpful rules in recalling the memory are:

- Using the **present tense.** Although it is in the past, recall it as if you are there now: 'I am enjoying the waves,' not 'I was enjoying the waves.'

- **Who** else (if anyone) is there – and their names.

- What you **see** there in as much detail as possible.

- What sounds you **hear** being here in this moment – is there any music, sounds of nature or the sounds of other people, or maybe just silence?

- What **feelings and sensations** you are aware of – in this case, the temperature of the water, how it feels as it washes over you, what the sand on the beach is like and so on.

By doing this you re-energize the precise pathways you used to create and store the feelings of that original experience, so re-triggering those pathways brings those feelings right back.

Just like Gordon and Brad, you'll need to step 'IN' to those memories in detail, it won't work just to recall them in some vague way, like 'beaches' or from watching it from some other perspective.

Avoid using phrases such as 'I am going to imagine that time', as imagining encourages the idea that you're making it up or pretending. And the same is true of 'remembering' as it makes it too much like a memory rather than something you're re-experiencing right now. A much better phrase is 'I am going to take myself back to'. So now each time you use the steps you go from:

- Asking and answering the question: 'What do you want?'

- To asking the question: 'And how are you going to get it?'

- Answering it by saying: 'I'm going to take myself back to…'

- Name the time you're returning to and then re-experience it in as much detail as possible.

This example is about having a 'deeply calm and confident' state, but the same structure applies for any 'state of mind' or 'state' that you want to get into. If you wish to be energized, you would choose to take yourself back to a time when you felt full of energy. If you wish to be focused, you would take yourself back to a time when you felt focused. If you wish to be motivated, you take yourself back to a time when you felt incredibly motivated to do something. The list and therefore the opportunities are endless.

Exercise: Pour it in

You can step IN to these feelings even more by using a powerful visualization technique. Choose a memory that fits the state that you want to create, reconnect with those powerful feelings, and then enhance them further by adding some sparkle and glow to them.

Ask yourself if those feelings were to have a colour, what colour would it be? Then have these feelings and let that colour just pour through you; and sense it flowing from your head through your body, down your arms and out of your hands, coursing through your spine and down through your legs, and flowing out of your feet.

Feel yourself being immersed in that, as you breathe it in deeply.

Re-score
Once you've accessed that great state and poured it into yourself re-score yourself out of 10, where 10 is feeling good and zero is not feeling good. Again you should notice a very significant improvement in your score.

Generally at this point you might expect to feel a score between eight and 10. Any less would indicate you need to go though some of the steps in this chapter again to raise you score, and increase the activation of the parts of the brain that you want on line, fired up and supporting you in your future.

Independent memories
You don't need to go back to a precisely matching time involving exactly the same situation or context. In other words, you don't need to recall a time of 'confidence when public speaking' in order to get in touch with the 'confidence' state you might need for speaking well in public. All you need to do is to go back to a time when you were confident. It really doesn't matter what the situation occurred in, because confidence is just confidence.

There aren't different types of confidence, one that you use for public speaking and one that you use somewhere else, they are all activations of exactly the same nerve pathways of confidence and so can be used in any situation in which you wish to feel confident.

One of the skills of this process is to be able to think creatively about times when you were in contact with exactly the feelings you wish to recreate. For example, many people say 'I've never been confident,' but when you ask them if they are confident that they can tie their shoelaces, tell the time, or if they've ever lived on Mars, they are supremely confident about these things.

These states of confidence are just as powerful as any others and can be used to generate confidence for any future situation. In fact, the same applies for *any* 'state' that we wish to get into.

Exercise: States

Take some time to consider what 'states', such as confidence, being energized, focused, motivated and so on, you would love to have more of in your life.

Also consider the catchphrases that take you into the Pit and what the opposite states would be to those versions of the Pit. So if you often dû stress then the opposite state would be calm; if you dû procrastination, the opposite state might be focused, motivated and proactive.

Having recognized the states you would like to have more of, make a list in your notebook of the times when you were in touch with these feelings. You might want to include photos from that time, or from tourist brochures or the website of a particular place. You can be creative in how you develop a deeper familiarity with these important memories.

Don't necessarily restrict yourself to going back to the same memories each time – so, for example, if one of your memories for calm is 'that beach in Mexico' you don't always have to go back to 'that beach in Mexico' to get in touch with calm. Some people find that by going back to the same experience time after time, they become bored with it. While others find it enhances and deepens their experience of it. Be guided by what works best for you.

Many people find that they have spent far too much time focusing on not very useful memories, and far too little time focusing on, or talking about, the really great things in their lives. We can see now that this is a really valuable thing to do for the health of your brain and for getting a life that you love. And now you know this you can take action to change your future by using your past more usefully.

Re-triggering

If you recall the story about the black VW Golf from an earlier chapter (*see page 117*) you'll remember how things and events in the world can trigger us to run destructive pathways, which make very little real-world logical sense – for example the trigger of 'seeing people playing golf' reminding me of 'my black VW Golf', which 'made me' upset.

There are things in the world that will continue to trigger those old negative pathways, but we can't remove all these triggers any more than I could forbid the driving of black VW Golfs while I was out in the street.

Luckily, this process is able to take advantage of these triggers in a new way.

Now every time a trigger event occurs that used to help you towards the Pit you will:

- Spot it.
- Stop it
- Choose to use your Coach and the two Coaching questions to get yourself into exactly the neurological state you desire.

Now the old triggered pathway has been rerouted, the trigger directly stimulates a great positive state, and things that used to bother you will now make you feel calm or smile.

And that is magical and life-changing.

Tips for the 'how?' question

There are four simple options for 'taking yourself back'. The first is as described above: finding an event in the past, which has all the feelings you need right now. However, sometimes people say, 'I just don't have a memory of a time when I felt that way,' which means you may need to spend a little longer thinking creatively about a time when you did have what you need in your memory bank. If, however, you still haven't located a memory of feeling that way then there are two other great options.

Role model

Choose someone who, for you, is a great role model of the state or quality that you wish to access. It can be:

- Someone you know.
- Someone you've heard or read about – a fictional character, e.g. Sherlock Holmes.
- An animal, or even an inanimate object, such as a tree, a rock or a mountain.

Imagine walking in their shoes for a day:

- Feeling what it feels like to be them.
- Thinking like them.
- Seeing the world through their eyes.
- Hearing themselves talking both out loud and to themselves.

Being creative in this way will give you a full sense of what it is like to live in the world with the qualities you admire in them. This works as well as accessing a positive memory because your brain can't distinguish easily between what really happened and what's imagination. So, developing this experience allows you to gain first-hand knowledge of what it feels like to have this quality.

Now, imagine pouring those qualities and approach to the world into yourself as you walk through today, operating as they would, thinking as they would, speaking as they would, enjoying the world as they would.

And any time you find yourself drifting from being that way use your Stop and the steps (*see page 178*) to get yourself back into that state; after all, it's what you want and you deserve it.

Future me

The other option is to take yourself into the future, when you have already achieved these changes, and feel what it feels like to be you in the future. In exactly the same way as using the 'role model' option above, walk in the shoes of your future self; pour those feelings into you, feeling how it feels to take on life in this way.

Exercise: Million-dollar me

This simple exercise can help you develop a new sense of your future self.

Imagine you've been given a huge amount of money (millions or billions, even) so that you can design somewhere that would naturally bring on these feelings that you wish for.

For example, imagine you wish to feel deeply relaxed, but have no good-quality memories to bring to mind.

With your unlimited budget you design the perfect place, so that when you're there you would naturally feel beautifully and deeply relaxed. Let's imagine a tropical island is your relaxation haven.

Have your living quarters be exactly the way you would love them to be, with all the design features you'd like. Money is no object, so it might have French windows with flowing white curtains opening onto a veranda, while an orchestra plays in a turquoise lagoon purely for your pleasure, and the fragrance of the tropical flowers is exactly how you imagined it to be...

Be creative – what would make it the most relaxing place in the world for you?

Tips for great states

Make sure you cover the basic points of being in the memory, creating it in great detail and using the present tense; as well as making sure, of course, that your voice and posture are congruent – matching the quality of that state.

Voice speed

Very often people speak too fast when they're trying to relax, too slowly and down when they're trying to re-energize themselves, so pace and volume are important.

Choose well

Make sure you choose a good memory, one that is powerful and evocative, and not mixed. For example, a relaxing memory of being snuggled up in bed in the morning won't be very positive if it's associated with an ex-partner with whom the relationship ended on bad terms.

Make sure the memory is 'clean' and that you're recalling it in a useful way rather than, for example, recalling a happy memory and then destroying it by remembering it being such a long time since you felt that way.

Both of these are examples of 'bad editing', which we'll be looking at more detail in a later chapter (*see page 249*).

For the moment, however, if you find yourself choosing either of these memory types, choose a different memory or recognize that you're unintentionally sneaking into the Pit, and then use your Stop and the steps (*see page 178*) to get yourself back on track.

You're a state-changing genius already

Above all, remember that you are really good at getting into states, it's a skill of yours – you, just like Gordon and Brad, are great at it. It just so happens you may have been practising getting into bad Pit states. Regardless of what kind of state you've been getting into, it reminds you just how good you are at it and so that means you **can** get into any state you choose.

Remember also, your brain doesn't really care which pathways you use. It will build itself around the most commonly used pathways, and so with practice these new states will become just as familiar and easy to access as those old negative ones that used to rule your life.

MAKING AN ACTION PLAN

Sometimes when you've worked out **what you want**, the solution to the second Coaching question – **'and how are you going to do that?'** – is very clear, as in this example:

Coach: 'What do you want?'

You: 'To go to the gym.'

Coach: 'How are you going to do that?'

You: 'I'm going to put my trainers on right now, and go.'

When you were in the Pit these kinds of choices just seemed unavailable to you, but when you're free from it, the solution is obvious. However, there are a few points worth covering in making sure your plan actually happens.

Time stamp

Make sure there is a 'by when' attached to this plan because saying, 'I'm going to go to gym' isn't enough to ensure it happens. Saying, 'I'm going to the gym this week' is better, but still quite vague and may slip your mind. So, the best answer to give is precise and specific. For example, 'I'm going to be at the gym by 1:20 p.m. today.'

This is much more likely to happen as the agreement you've made with yourself is very clear. You can make it certain to occur by putting it in your diary right now. Why not take even better care of yourself from now on and start making appointments with yourself, just as you would do with anybody else that is important?

Check it's reasonable

Just consider whether you have enough time in your schedule to make this action plan happen. If not, then either reschedule the gym trip or one of the other events in your diary to make room for it. Thinking through your action plan now will save you dûing stress about not having fulfilled your commitment, or trying to fit too many things into the same time slot.

Tell others about your plan

Letting other people know that this is what is going to be happening tends to make it more real. Tell someone you know who will help keep you on track and can share in your sense of success when you achieve that.

Re-score

Once you've made your action plan re-score yourself out of 10, where 10 is feeling good and zero is not feeling good. Again you should notice a significant improvement in your score.

Finally, you'll also find that even if you decide that your answer to this question is going to be a plan, it's usually incredibly useful to make sure you're in the right state to make that plan happen.

If you combine these two approaches you will end up going to the gym by putting your trainers on and leaving the house at the right time (the plan), and feeling motivated to do so (the state) by getting fully into that state. This way, suddenly life just starts to work better and you have a formula for success:

A great plan plus great state truly revolutionizes lives.

ACTION

This, again, is a great place to pause as you've now integrated the main elements of the training. Now every time you spot the Pit, you should Stop and Choose to Coach yourself. As the Coach, you acknowledge and ask the two questions, 'What do you want?' and 'How are you going to get that?'

The answer to this second question will take you into a great state and might be combined with an action plan, which will change how you feel. Feeling positive, motivated, relaxed and happy activates the great pathways of your brain and moves you into a life you love, NOW.

When you're ready continue to the next section, which is all about how to make all this work 'stick' neurologically.

PART III
Resilience

*Using the steps kindly, compassionately
and appropriately will result in huge
changes in your life.*

Part III considers the practical aspects of using these ideas;
and works through techniques to ensure that you're getting
the best neurological change for having the life you love, NOW.

CHAPTER 1

Lesson 18: Reflection Position, End and Overview

Having moved away from the Pit, by re-routing your brain to access great states and life-affirming pathways, you are now well on the way to getting a life you love NOW.

You don't have to use this final step every time but it can be a useful place to pause, after you've got yourself out of the Pit and back on track. Welcome to the place of Reflection.

Here you get a fresh perspective on the process that you've just been through, so that you can learn from the experience. In this place, just pause and ask yourself:

What have I learned from this that is really useful for my future?

This question allows your brain to start to 'generalize' the change you have experienced. To understand this step, imagine you've used the steps of the process on 'being (dûing) stressed at work'; and, successfully, calmed yourself down, so that you now feel deeply peaceful. In this place of Reflection, you may realize that you've now learned, 'If I can do this at the office, then I can do it anywhere – at home, at the supermarket, in crowds.'

This step of the process allows your brain to figure out exactly how useful this change is going to be. It makes this change more rapid by developing new pathways, ready to adopt these new ways of thinking, and installing new behaviours, ready for use in all sorts of different contexts in your life.

Reflection is also where you can consider the Pit from a safe distance, learning to recognize it even more clearly. You may remember I mentioned that, sometimes, you can find yourself in the Pit, without even knowing what you said to yourself to make it happen? So, this is a chance to look back over the events that helped you into the Pit; and consider, 'How did that happen?' or 'What did I say, do or think to get myself there?'

When you're in the Pit there's always a reason; it doesn't 'just' occur randomly or passively. As we saw with the ELFs (Excellences of Limited Function), there's an active mechanism and structure behind every journey we take into the Pit. Reflection, therefore, is your opportunity to see which ticket you bought.

THE END OF THE PROCESS

With any process there's a starting point (in this case, spotting the Pit, taking the steps towards your goal) and an end point. So, how do you know when it is time to finish?

The answer is quite simple; use the process steps kindly, compassionately and appropriately until you've got yourself out of the Pit. So, for example, if recognizing stress starts the process then it ends when you are calm.

Once you're accustomed to doing the process you'll be able to run through it, from stress to calm, in about 15 seconds. And the calmness will continue to be there, unless you start heading towards the Pit again.

OVERVIEW

And, with that, we've reached the end of the basic steps of how to get a life you love, right NOW. There are a few advanced additions, which will follow, to make using the process easier.

At this stage, it is really useful to remind yourself of the seven steps of the process; after all, they are the foundations of everything else.

REFLECTION IS YOUR **OPPORTUNITY** TO SEE WHICH **TICKET** YOU BOUGHT.

In the last few chapters, they've been covered in great detail, so that you are well versed in how to use them properly. But, in spite of the number of pages it has taken to describe them accurately, the actual steps are designed to be really quite simple.

1. Present	
2. Spot the Pit	Quickly score yourself out of 10, where 10 is feeling good and zero is not feeling good
3. Stop	Choose the appropriate one
4. Choice	Ask, 'That way or this way?'
5. Coach	Acknowledge – check we have taken it in and re-score Ask, 'What do you want?' Answer and re-score Ask, 'and how are you going to get it?' Answer by either taking yourself back to a time when you felt that way and/or creating an action plan – re-score
6. End	By recognizing you are now Present again and creating a life you love
7. Reflection	Ask, 'What have I learned from this, that is really useful for my future?'

Of course, this process, of the apparently simplistic seven steps, is ineffective without an understanding of, among other things, the power of genius, posture, congruence, the language of change and how neuroplasticity is a powerful tool to be used carefully. However, combining these steps appropriately and compassionately with this understanding will result in huge changes in your life.

PRACTICAL ISSUES
Now you have a solid understanding of the steps, there are some important points to make about how to put them into practice in the real world.

Do I do the steps out loud and with the movements?

This question was covered in an earlier chapter (*see page 147*), but now you have more steps let's recap.

My experience is that, in the early stages, doing it physically and out loud is best, if possible. At times when you're not sure whether or not it would be appropriate, there are a number of options:

- Do it anyway... let people think what they think, but where you do it is your call.

- Take yourself somewhere private and use the process.

- Once you've spotted the Pit, do it on your hand – holding your thumb and one finger at a time in this order:
  - » Thumb – Stop
  - » First finger – Choice
  - » Second finger – Coach acknowledge
  - » Third finger – Ask, 'What do you want?' And 'How are you going to get it?'
  - » Fourth finger – Take myself back

- During a conversation: doing the steps will bring you back more fully to the conversation.

Should I tell others I'm working through this book?

The answer depends on whether they would be supportive or not. Some people will be great allies and assist you while others may be cynical, critical or try and undermine you, so choose which people you enlist in your support team carefully. If you have a partner then it's probably good to explain the new ways of thinking that you're going to be putting into practice, but it's up to you!

Additionally, Lesson 21 (*see page 237*) will answer many of the other questions that might arise while using the Process.

KEY POINTS FOR YOUR WORKBOOK

Throughout the book there have been a number of places where I've recommended that you note down your responses in your workbook; however, out of all of them, these are the most valuable ones:

- **Successes:** These are the times when you've used the process to get change. This will be really useful for the 'editing' exercise (*see page 252*) you'll be doing daily for the next two weeks.

- **Catchphrases:** Write these down as you notice them (*see page 144*) as they provide an early warning system that you're heading into the Pit and need to use the process now.

- **Stuck:** Anytime you didn't get the changes you hoped for; this will be particularly useful for the chapters that follow on ways to deal with such moments.

SET GOALS

As you'll discover, particularly in the following chapters on editing, noticing changes and celebrating them, setting goals is an important part of creating new positive nerve pathways. In order to assist this, choose some goals you'd really love to achieve using these steps. Just remember to make your goals:

- **Reasonable:** For example, if presenting in front of a small group is currently something you dû scared about, then it's probably not a good idea to take on appearing in front of thousands at this point, unless you feel up for it…

- **Different:** Choose a goal that you can see as a clear achievement. You don't want to achieve something that you could later easily undermine by saying, 'Well, I probably could have done that anyway.'

You're looking for something you can easily recognise as something to celebrate. Fortunately, the next chapter explores a key method for rapidly speeding up your brain's familiarity with these new ways of thinking.

CHAPTER 2

Lesson 19: Brain Rehearsal and Step-by-step Examples

By this point, no doubt you understand how much work is required in the process, but also how often conversations (with yourself and others) are in danger of leading you headlong into the Pit. However, this doesn't mean that you'll have to use the steps endlessly for everything, for three main reasons:

1. The more you use your new brain pathways, the more exercised and automatic they become and, before long, the steps will seem to run automatically (just in the same way the old routes to the Pit seemed to be on autopilot).

2. As you resolve some of your old ways of thinking, which may have been messing up your life for years, many other problems will fade away. If you stop being stressed, for example, it will naturally increase your self-esteem and confidence. Uncomfortable situations, which used to be difficult, will no longer be off limits. In this way, the change becomes 'generative', where changing one thing has an impact on another issue. This is one of those constructive, rather than destructive, spirals mentioned earlier (*see page 99*).

3. Finally, there's an invaluable additional step to the process, which grows and strengthens the pathways into the life you love, called 'Brain Rehearsal'.

BRAIN REHEARSAL

When Brad and Gordon prepared for their interviews, you'll have noticed that they predicated a future based on their past. Although these sorts of predictions are powerful, they aren't always accurate or useful. The brain also has a 'weighting' system, whereby it gives certain memories more significance. This system seems to be influenced by:

- How recently an event occurred or the memory was accessed.
- How many events occurred.
- How strongly emotive they were.
- How much of an effect they had on you.

Just because the last interviewer was unpleasant doesn't mean they all will be. Yet, the emotional significance and recentness of this event makes the feelings of the 'nasty interviewer' stronger and more influential in our decision-making. And, just because the memory is recent or emotionally important, or often recalled, it can skew our version of what's likely to happen in the future.

During this process, we consider the likely negative consequences of the bad interview by stepping into that future prediction. As soon as we do this, we create a **memory** about the future!

In turn, this creates a whole series of bad *memories* about what's going to happen, and generates huge levels of nervous anxiety about an event, which doesn't even currently exist.

Central to this memory weighting system is that the brain doesn't seem to be able to distinguish very well between attaching emotions to events that *have* happened and events that *will/ might* happen. We can feel the same degree of strong emotional response to both, as anyone who's ever been stressed about a forthcoming event can testify.

However, you can also use this same predictive process very effectively for good by creating a set of powerful memories of the future being great, which leads your brain to expect and predict good things for that future.

Using all the steps

Let's go through an example of using all the steps and adding Brain Rehearsal on to the end of the process to deepen the activation of the neurology of change.

Pit – score

The Pit begins with, for example, 'I am really stressed about a forthcoming presentation.' This brings on some unpleasant feelings and in terms of feeling good, scores two out of 10.

Stop

Insert a calm Stop, to counteract ' dûing stress': 'I am… Stop.'

Choice

Ask, 'That way or this way?' Then step into being a Coach.

Coach

Give authentic, congruent and calm acknowledgement, saying:

- 'Well done! You're on track.'
- 'You are a powerful genius.'
- 'You can do anything you put your mind to.'
- 'I will be with you every single step of the way.'
- 'I love you and admire you.'
- 'You deserve great things.'
- 'Everything is going to be okay.'

Present – re-score

Step into the Present, checking that we have taken in the acknowledgement, and re-score – getting a higher score than before.

Coach – first question

Step back into the Coach position and ask the first question: 'What do you want?'

Present – re-score
Step back to the Present and, for example, answer: 'I want to be deeply calm and serene during the presentation, like a mountain stream flowing over rocks and boulders.'

This is a great answer. Re-score – getting a higher score than before (e.g. six out of 10).

Coach – Second question
The Coach asks, 'And how are you going to do that?'

Present – take myself back
Step into the Present again and answer, for example, 'by taking myself back to that time when I felt really confident speaking in front of all my friends and family at my parents' wedding anniversary dinner.' Become immersed in that experience, letting the colour of the memory flow throughout the body.

Re-score
Score is now nine out of 10.

Completing the standard steps means you'll feel much more confident about the presentation and by doing the additional Brain Rehearsal step will make those feelings even more powerful and those pathways even stronger.

The Brain Rehearsal step
In this step, take yourself into the future to a time distant enough from now that you can be very confident you'll have made the changes you desire; a time so far in the future that those changes will now seem commonplace and completely normal to you.

This part of the process is outlined below, with the example of going five years into the future.

- Standing in the Present, take yourself five years into the future.

- Remind yourself that with the passing of time you'll be very good at using these tools, and will have completely achieved your goal many times over.

  » In this scenario, you'll have aced dozens of presentations.

- Fill in some of the details of the positive experiences that must have happened to get there.

  » For example, you'll have worked successfully with big and small crowds, friendly audiences and ones you had to win over, people who were interested in what you were saying and audiences who were less up for it; you have such a wealth of successful, positive experiences of dealing with all these variables that presentations are now easy, simple and normal for you.

- How does it feel as you do that thing one more time in five years and one day's time?

  » For example, walking on stage for yet another presentation in five years and one day's time.

- Step IN to that successful movie, fully detailing:

  » What you see.

  » What you hear, both in your confident head and from the audience.

  » And how it feels to be confident in that situation with all those years of experience behind you.

- Now, imagine you have a hosepipe and, when you turn it on, those feelings flood out from the 'you five years in the future', arcing through time and flooding into the 'you of today'. What colours do those feelings have? Feel what it would be like to absorb those feelings.

- Re-score out of 10, where 10 is feeling great. Notice how you feel about the forthcoming situation when you have complete access to those feelings of five years in the future, as you walk through it now.

HOW IT WORKS

When you take yourself into this successful future, five years from now, your brain fills in the intervening years with 'memories' that fit with that successful end event – in this example, the feeling of 'I have years of experience of being successful with presentations.'

Creating all these memories and fully immersing yourself in that successful future instantly exercises and strengthens your positive nerve pathways. This affects the 'weighting' (*see page 208*) of how the brain calculates what's likely to happen in the future.

As a result, when your brain now considers presentations, it suddenly has a wealth of very positive, recent and powerful experiences of being successful in that environment.

It's irrelevant that these memories have only just been generated by the Brain Rehearsal step of the process. So, it predicts and prepares for confidence and success, by connecting up the nerve pathways of confidence and success with the nerve pathways of presentations.

As you'll remember, 'nerves that fire together, wire together', so now the pathways of success, confidence and presentations all start to be physically connected to each other. This means, instead of having to do the steps of the process to feel good in presentations, the good feelings are already waiting for you whenever you think about, or actually get to, the presentation experience itself.

Brain Rehearsal is very effective because it simply utilizes that successful prediction process, which already works so well for becoming 'nervous' about the future. That process is excellent at producing very strong feelings in advance, and can switch them on instantaneously when you get into the situation itself. If it's so good at producing anxiety and stress, it will be equally brilliant at producing great feelings too.

THE **POWER** OF YOUR **IMAGINATION** TO DIRECTLY **CREATE** YOUR FUTURE IS **IMMENSE;** USE IT **WISELY.**

Exercise: Brain Rehearsal

Now take an issue and use the standard steps (shown on page 209), then conclude with the Brain Rehearsal step.

- How did that enhance your experience of your future success?

WHEN TO USE IT

You won't need to use this advanced technique every time, but it's invaluable in situations where you wish to get the life you love but know you won't be able to do the process at the time. For example, it would look a bit odd to get up and do the process steps in a cinema, restaurant or at work.

It's also a really useful way of preparing in advance for any forthcoming events or scenarios. So set aside a little time every day for the first few weeks to run through any upcoming situations that you want to deal with from a better state than you have in the past. Just a few minutes' preparation, setting the brain pathways heading in the right direction, can save you hours of using the process in the actual situation itself.

DEALING WITH OTHERS

One particularly useful application of the process is that it can help us deal with those people in our lives that, without meaning, really help and encourage us into the Pit.

You'll know by now they can't *make* you go into the Pit, but they can help – and some seem to be geniuses at it. Unfortunately, often they are people we can't avoid, e.g. family members, work colleagues, customers, in-laws, etc.

You can't change them, and they're likely to continue to be the same way for some time. You may even find that, as you make changes and they no longer get the response they expect, they 'turn up the volume' of their behaviours to try to get the response they used to get. With time, this will change, as it takes two to cause an argument or difficult situation, and eventually they will give up when they realize that you're not joining in any more.

But let's get back to the solution first, and consider the classic sitcom example of a difficult relationship with a mother-in-law. She is someone that you dû irritation around; she seems to know exactly the right thing to say to make you behave in ways that you regret (mostly) afterwards. So, let's work through this scenario to see how we deal with it using the steps of the process.

Pit – score
The Pit begins with thinking, for example, *GRRRRR. She is really annoying me now.* This brings some unpleasant feelings and in terms of feeling good, scores two out of 10.

Stop
Insert a calm Stop, to counteract 'dûing annoyance': '*GRR*Stop.'

Choice
Ask, 'That way or this way?' Then step into being a Coach.

Coach
Give authentic, congruent and calm acknowledgement, saying:

- 'Well done! You're on track.'
- 'You are a powerful genius.'
- 'You can do anything you put your mind to.'
- 'I will be with you every single step of the way.'
- 'I love you and admire you.'
- 'You deserve great things.'
- 'Everything is going to be okay.'

Present – re-score
Step into the Present, acknowledge and re-score – getting a higher score than before.

Coach – first question
Step back to the Coach and ask the first question: 'What do you want?'

Present – re-score
Step back to the Present and, for example, answer: 'I want to be **relaxed and happy**, independent of what **she** does, like a duck in the rain.'

This is great: it's positive, something you can deliver and stated in 'big' language. Re-score – getting about seven out of 10 now.

Coach – second question
The Coach asks, 'And how are you going to do that?'

Present – take myself back
Step into the Present again and answer: 'By taking myself back to that time on the beach in Mexico... I am feeling really relaxed and happy on the beach.' Become immersed in that feel-good experience, letting its colour flow throughout the whole body.

Another great answer for these kinds of situations is by taking yourself back to a time when you were able to be with someone who wasn't saying what you wanted to hear but you were fine with it.

Examples might include: children who say they hate you, simply because you won't give them a second ice cream; or hearing a slightly crazed, homeless guy shouting that you're really a paperclip from the planet Venus.

How do you feel in these kinds of situations?

Re-score
Score is now nine out of 10.

Brain Rehearsal
The final additional Brain Rehearsal step will make these feelings even more powerful and those pathways even stronger.

- Standing in the Present, take yourself five years into the future.

216

- Remind yourself that with the passing of time you will so be good at using these tools, and will have completely achieved your goal many times over.

  » In this scenario, you will have got really used to being like a duck in the rain around her.

- Fill in some of the details of the positive experiences that must have happened to get there.

  » For example, you will have been happy around her when she's bored, talking, moaning, happy, gossiping etc. You now have such a wealth of successful, positive experiences of dealing with all these variables that being with her and being calm is easy for you. How does it feel as you do that thing one more time in five years and one days' time?

- Step IN to that successful movie, fully detailing:

  » What you see.

  » What you hear, both in your confident head and from your mother-in-law.

  » And how it feels to be confident in that situation with all those years of experience behind you.

- Now, imagine you have a hosepipe and, when you turn it on, those feelings flood out from the 'you five years in the future', arcing over time and flooding into the 'you of today'. What colours do those feelings have? Feel what it would be like to absorb those feelings.

- Re-score out of 10, where 10 is feeling great. Notice how you feel about the forthcoming situation you've been using this process for (in this case, the next time she is due to visit), when you have complete access to those feelings of five years in the future as you walk through it now.

You can see how powerful this additional step will be in making these changes stick and reducing the amount of time you'll need to spend doing the steps of the process. Working with your brain in this way will ensure it is well rehearsed to expect success in any given situation.

The next few chapters look at ways of putting these skills into practice, special situations that might need additional insight and advanced tools.

Let's start with one of the most important, 'beliefs'.

CHAPTER 3

Lesson 20: Beliefs – Hidden Powers

While writing this chapter, I realized that in every single book I've written so far, there has been a section or chapter on beliefs. However, that's not very surprising because beliefs are one of the most powerful forces in our lives. They guide us, inspire us, make us do extraordinary things or keep us stuck; we fight for them and some die for them.

The biggest problem with beliefs is that most of the time we don't even notice their presence. This is because when we have a belief about something we actually think we are dealing with facts, true explanations of how the world works, rather than just a set of opinions that we have somehow chosen to buy into.

The beliefs we've ended up with are the result of a long process of consideration, as they are our attempt to get the best possible understanding we can of the world. If we have come to an opinion about how the world works, it's because we've examined the evidence over time, sought out others' opinions, and come to a logical conclusion, based on the evidence we've found.

THE CHANGEABILITY AND STAYING POWER OF BELIEFS

Yet, history is littered with well-known examples of beliefs held with absolute certainty by the majority of the population and the most prestigious academics of the time – and still these well-held beliefs came tumbling down, when new evidence finally overturned them. And I say *finally* because very often a well-established belief will continue to keep its grip on being the 'only version of truth', even when there is a wealth of information that says it's outdated. It often takes a very long time for old established beliefs to change.

A classic example is the Ptolemaic, and Christian, view that the universe rotated around the Earth. It sounds crazy now, but when Galileo discovered evidence that the sun was the centre of the solar system, and our Earth was not, it is said that he was threatened with excommunication and death for preaching heresy. So, what can we learn from this?

- Beliefs affect how we see things as being right or wrong, depending on whether it fits with the belief.

- The longer a belief has existed the more evidence it has to support itself, and yet the more likely it is to have become outdated.

- Beliefs can cause blind bigotry, where we are just not open to looking at other perspectives.

- Beliefs change; even the most established and widely held ones are subject to change.

Exercise: Recognizing beliefs

Use this exercise to see how successful you are at distinguishing between opinions or beliefs and facts. For this exercise, consider a 'fact' to be something that can be documented in some way and 'beliefs or opinions' to be something that some people think is true, but not everyone agrees with.

1. A bat and ball cost £1.10. If the bat costs £1 more than the ball then what does the ball cost? If I tell you the answer is not 10 pence, would you believe me?

2. There are more humans in the world than chickens. Belief or fact?

3. Two plus two is an easy sum that equals four. Belief or fact?

4. George Washington was the first and most influential president of the USA. Belief or fact?

5. When the two planes crashed into the World Trade Center on 9/11 it was a bad thing because over 2,500 people died as a result. Belief or fact?

The answers

1. In this question[9] most people will have worked out that the ball obviously costs 10 pence, and I must be mistaken. Let's look at the maths behind this. If the ball did cost 10 pence – as most people think – and the bat was £1, the difference between the cost of the bat and ball is 90 pence, so it can't be correct as the question said the difference was £1 and not 90 pence. In fact, as the total for the two items is £1.10, the answer is the ball must cost 5 pence, because then the bat would have cost the remaining £1.05, making the difference between the cost of the bat and the ball the required £1. However, some people will need to go through this section a few times to be completely convinced of its correctness. Not because it's complicated maths – it's clearly not – but just because we are noticing a conflict between what we were certain the right answer should be (our belief, which we doubt is wrong) and how that is 'apparently different' from the correct answer.

2. This is a much simpler question for most people to answer; it's a belief, as it's not factually accurate. In fact there are more chickens than humans in the world. This is something you either know or don't know. Unless you previously had researched this fact, you would have had a belief about which was correct or incorrect, you're probably not that concerned either way, and if you got it wrong you are probably quite happy to change your belief about it.

3. This statement is false. Although it is accurate that two plus two equals 4, notice it is combined with the statement 'this is an easy sum'. This second part is not accurate; most babies, for example, wouldn't find this easy and so the whole statement becomes false. In the same way

as someone saying, 'Whales are mammals that swim in the sea and are the size of a pea,' simply because two thirds of the statement is correct doesn't make a whole sentence true.

4. George Washington was, of course the first President of the USA, so that portion of the statement is factual, but saying 'he was the most influential president' is, however, an opinion, as influence cannot be measured in any standardized way. Although it may well be an opinion that many people hold, there are bound to be some people in the street or in the White House, or academics, who might argue that other presidents were more or equally influential, such as Lincoln, Kennedy or Roosevelt. All these would be reasonable opinions.

5. Many people in the West will consider this to be fact, but it's not. Certain elements of it are factual – the planes did crash into the World Trade Center on 9/11 and over 2,500 people died as a result. However, the statement that it was 'a bad thing' is an opinion. It may be an opinion that you, most of the readers of this book and I share, but we also know that there was celebration in certain parts of the world when the events were broadcast. So although we may think this is a bad thing, it is not a 'bad' thing in everybody's opinion. And so this portion of the statement makes it an opinion or belief.

How did you do? Five out of five?

I'm guessing (I have a belief about it) that most people will trip up on one or more of these questions, and that's pretty common. We don't seem to be great at being able to distinguish 'opinions or beliefs' from facts.

And this is very important, as your beliefs serve as your current blueprint or set of rules about who you are, what you are capable of and how the world works.

If you can't distinguish your opinions from the actual facts about how you, or the world is, then you risk getting suckered into thinking you have a good and complete understanding of things, which may be completely wrong.

THE **PROBLEM** WITH **BELIEFS** IS THAT WE **MISTAKE** THEM FOR **FACTS.**

GOLDEN RULE OF BELIEFS

Clearly, our beliefs have a massive influence on our levels of success, fulfilment and happiness. Luckily, there are only three main things we need to do with them to move our life on:

• Spot the beliefs at work in our lives.

• Use the Golden Rule of Beliefs, which means realizing that the question we need to ask of beliefs, probably surprisingly, is not are they right or wrong, but whether they are:

 » Destructive, limiting and negative;

 » Or **useful** and move us towards a life we love.

• And if they aren't useful then we need to use the steps below to change them.

THE USEFULNESS OF BELIEFS

Some time ago, I decided to believe that everything is simple and easy. Do you share that belief or think that some things are easy and others more difficult?

Just to be clear, my belief is not actually a true or accurate version of the way the world really is; it is just a belief that I choose to believe.

Why do I do that?

It makes me happier and more successfully productive, and the world more interesting. It's definitely changed the lives of thousands, as it was core to my approach to finding solutions to illnesses that were medically considered to be 'impossible to recover from'. So I believe it's just fundamentally much more useful to think that way.

Let's take the example of nuclear physics – the study of the component parts of atoms. Is that a simple or difficult subject to grasp?

Many people would argue it is a difficult subject. However, as I believe everything is simple and easy, why should nuclear physics be any different?

Imagine if I found an amazing teacher, who was an expert in the field, who could entertain and engage me while teaching me everything there was to learn about the subject; making it fun by throwing pies to demonstrate how electrons move within the atom, and enjoying the discussions and debates within the field. As I believe there is no 'magic', no unteachable secrets, along the way, eventually if I kept on that course, being open and available to the teaching, I would learn everything my expert teacher knew about nuclear physics. At that point nuclear physics would be simple for me. So is nuclear physics a simple or difficult subject to grasp?

The answer is that it's neither; the difficulty or simplicity comes from a combination of you and your teacher's attitudes, beliefs and behaviours, not from the subject itself.

Once again, it's mainly all down to our beliefs. If we think it's hard, it will be; if we think it's very easy, so it will be and our behaviours will follow from that.

If we think that something is going to be hard, then either we won't start it or become disheartened when we come across the first obstacle, and give up, as we knew there would be an impossibility along the road.

If, instead, we start by thinking it's going to be simple, when we meet the first obstacle, we take it on as an intriguing challenge; and start to work out a way round it, knowing there *has* to be a way around because learning this is simple.

The question to ask is not, 'Is it hard or easy?' But, 'Which belief is more useful for learning?'

To answer this question, let's look at how to spot beliefs and how to change the ones that don't fit the Golden Rule.

SPOTTING BELIEFS

There are a number of ways to notice the presence of beliefs; the simplest is by becoming much more aware of your language.

It is this way

Watch out for any statement beginning with the following:

- 'She/he/it IS...'
- 'I AM...'
- 'They/you ARE...'

which then goes on to express an idea of 'this way'.

- 'I am... ugly, etc.'
- 'It is... difficult to...'

These kinds of statements usually express beliefs about the way you think the world is.

Predictions
Will/won't

Any statement about 'what is likely to happen' is fundamentally a belief, because as the future event hasn't happened yet we can't possibly **know** what is going to happen. We only have predictions based on what happened last time. You'll spot this in statements beginning with:

- 'He/she/it/they/etc. WILL/WON'T...'

In certain mechanical areas of science it is reasonable to make predictions based on what was observed to happen in the past. For example, if we kick a ball, we know that if we repeat our kick, accurately, keeping the same speed and angle, we can predict where the ball will end up.

There are such few variables in this 'simple' system that it's reasonable to apply this kind of thinking to this situation.

If, however, we replace the ball with a gorilla, the outcome is much less predictable. This is because now we are dealing with a much more complex system, where the gorilla has a number of potential responses to being kicked.

Can't

A special, and especially common, example of predictions is 'can't'. Any statement that includes the idea of:

- 'I can't.'

- 'It can't be done.'

- 'It can only be that way.'

- 'It's impossible.'

This is, again, making a prediction about the future and, specifically, saying it's just not possible. An example would be to say, 'I can't be confident in interviews.'

This is a prediction that 'something is just not possible', which is neither useful nor life-enhancing. If you continue to buy into 'I can't', it will continue to be true; however, if you choose to let go of it then it gives you the chance to make changes to your behaviour. Without letting go of that belief first there's no possibility of change, as why would you bother putting any energy into trying to change something that you know is impossible?

It's worth pointing out that not all beliefs about what's possible are bad. We can see this by applying the Golden Rule – 'Is it useful and does it enhance your life?' For example, 'I can't jump off this roof and fly' is a good example of a life-enhancing and useful belief.

It's not a question of changing all beliefs, just changing the ones that are not useful and don't enhance your life.

All

Another great way to spot the presence of beliefs is to notice generalizations. In other words, where we say the world, or some of its components, is *all* a particular way. Examples are:

- 'ALL men/women are…'

- 'People like me NEVER get promoted.'

They can be spotted by the presence of the words listed earlier in the chapter on ELFs (Excellences of Limited Function; *see page 29*):

- 'Every time…'

- 'All…'

- 'Never...'
- 'Always...'
- 'Each time...'
- 'As usual...'
- 'Forever...'
- Nobody/no one, etc.'

Often the word will be 'silent' in such statements as:

- 'Women can't park', actually means 'all women can't park'.
- 'Snakes are dangerous', actually means 'all snakes are dangerous'.

So, listen out for any sweeping statements inferring that this is ALWAYS true in ALL cases.

Ought and should

The following words will usually show up the presence of a belief, usually concerning a sense of guilt, attempting to keep someone else happy or to comply with another person's rules:

- 'I have to...'
- 'I need to...'
- 'I ought to...'
- 'I must...'
- 'I should...'

Examples are:

- 'I have to be hard on myself.'
- 'I should think of others before myself.'
- 'I mustn't enjoy myself too much.'
- 'I ought not to say how I really feel.'
- 'I shouldn't say, "I'm good at this."'

Exercise: Your beliefs

Write down your answer to the following question.

• What limiting beliefs do you now notice you've been holding onto, which you need to let go of to get a life you love?

THE COST OF LIMITING BELIEFS

In my books *The Introduction to the Lightning Process* and *Dû – Unlock Your Full Potential With A Word,* there are large sections on the power of beliefs over our health. I'll just share two very brief but fascinating stories here that emphasize how incredibly powerful beliefs are.

Placebos and traditions

In a blind controlled drugs trial[10], comparing the effects of chemotherapy to taking a dummy pill (a placebo), in which neither group knew if they were taking the real pill or the placebo, a stunning finding was uncovered.

The group who were taking the real chemotherapy lost, as would be expected, most of their body hair. However, in the group taking the dummy pill, 30 per cent of them also lost all their body hair – the hair on their head, their eyebrows and eyelashes.

What was responsible for them losing their hair, when the pill they were taking contained no active substances whatsoever?

It was their beliefs.

Another researcher, D.P. Phillips, at the University of California, studied Chinese families who had moved to the USA. It was recognized that some families kept with their traditions, while others became completely westernized.

The more traditional families saw the importance of the traditional Chinese system of understanding the world (e.g. the power of the five elements of fire, earth, metal, water and wood) on their health. According to this traditional Chinese medicine, if a person is born in a 'metal' year, defined by their astrological chart, they would be more likely to have lung problems in later life.

When death rates in Chinese families in the USA were analysed, it was found that if a person was born in the year of 'metal' and had become westernized they had no more chance than any other US citizen of dying of lung-related illness. But, amazingly, if they were born in a 'metal' year and raised in a 'traditional' Chinese family they would have an increased chance of dying of lung-related illness.

Again, what caused this effect?

The hidden power of beliefs.

So, you can see that, once you've distinguished any limiting beliefs, it's vital to change them as, if they can do this, they can be very effective at preventing the change you want from happening in any part of your life.

THE LIFECYCLE OF BELIEFS

The first step in changing beliefs is to realize that you were not born with them. You generated and built them – often with help from outside experts, especially your parents, teachers and peers – and, as time went on, you modified them.

There is an interesting question I often ask about beliefs which is:

Are beliefs easy or difficult to change?

People will vary in their answers to this question. Some say they are difficult to change, while others will say some are difficult to change and others are slightly easier, and the rare few will say beliefs are easy to change.

What's interesting is these are their beliefs about how easy or difficult it is to change a belief! Unfortunately, as we've already identified, if you have a belief that it is difficult to change beliefs, then it will be. Equally, if you have a belief that it is easy to change beliefs, that will be too.

One of the things that changes a belief the most is seeing clear evidence yourself that the way you think the world is may not be entirely accurate. So let's start with some evidence about how easy it is to change beliefs, because if you wish to change beliefs, then this is probably the first one to start with.

Father Christmas

Now I don't want to spoil anyone's Christmas, and if you're under 10 please skip this section, but... Father Christmas isn't real.

Many people can remember the moment when they discovered this upsetting truth. For me, it was as a five-year-old talking to my big sister, who was a whole two years older than me and therefore incredibly wise.

I can still remember when she told me who it really was. I remember doubting her; after all I'd seen him on TV and at the shopping mall with his elves. She had to be wrong. But she kept on insisting this was true, and she was wise and always right about things, and she said it with such conviction that within a few moments life was never the same again.

And that is how quickly beliefs can change.

A client of mine told me it happened to them when they were 12 and their English teacher set them the task of writing an essay titled, 'When I found out Father Christmas wasn't real'. That's a tough way to find out!

Exercise: Changed beliefs

When did you experience this kind of shift in belief from 'this is the way it is' to 'that probably isn't true' or 'this just isn't true'?

If you can't remember that Father Christmas revelation moment from your childhood, choose a different example, the tooth fairy maybe...

Or having a pinup, who you imagined would at one point stroll into your classroom and whisk you away to spend the rest of their life with you...

Or that you were destined to represent your country at sport/gymnastics/the Olympics...

Or, maybe, it's looking back at the clothes you used to wear in your teens and how 'cool' you knew they were, but now when you look at them, you can't quite see how you ever wore them...

The intriguing fact is that we change thousands of beliefs without even thinking about it throughout our life. I'll never:

- Get a girl/boyfriend.
- Get a degree.
- Learn to master driving a car.
- Be able to tie my shoelaces.
- Learn to tell the time.
- Be able to count up to 100.

And so on. When you look at it you can see that we are very experienced geniuses at changing beliefs, we just tend to do it without actively thinking about it.

WHO'S IN CHARGE OF OUR BELIEFS?

Most of our beliefs are formed when we encounter an authority figure who shows or tells us how the world really works. We will either accept their wisdom blindly, or consider it as a reputable source of information and start to see the world from that perspective.

However, although other people often 'helped' us design these beliefs about the world, they are now rarely authority figures in our lives, yet we still carry those beliefs forwards.

When you think about it, it's only 'us' who are continuing to sell ourselves this belief. This is great news because if we are in charge of our beliefs then we can choose to dump the ones we don't want or need any more.

Changing beliefs

Fortunately you can use the steps that you've learned in this book to make exactly this change, simply and easily. Let's work through that using an example:

Pit – score

'It is not okay to be nice to myself.'

Start by assessing the strength of the belief **you would like to have:** 'It is okay to be nice to myself.' Score yourself out of 10, where 10 is 'I completely agree' and zero is 'I do not agree at all'. Whatever your answer is at this point is fine, just note it down, so you can see how much and how fast it changes.

Stop

Now use the Stop, and then move to the position of Choice. Pause in this position a little longer than usual.

Choice

Here you look at the consequences of continuing to hold onto and nurture this belief. After all, we are, somehow, choosing to keep this belief alive – or dûing the belief.

Make a choice to give yourself permission to let go of this and fully replace it with something more useful and life-affirming. If you find this choice difficult it means you have another belief, possibly about deserving to have a great life; however, for the purpose of this example let's imagine that you have made a clear choice that you want to move on in your life and let this belief go.

Coach

Step into the Coach position and acknowledge yourself for making a great choice. Say the important acknowledgement phrases of the Coach:

- 'Well done! You're on track.'

- 'You are a powerful genius.'

- 'You can do anything you put your mind to.'

- 'I will be with you every single step of the way.'

- 'I love you and admire you.'

- 'You deserve great things.'

- 'Everything is going to be okay.'

Present – re-score

Step into the square of the Present, and make sure you've listened to your Coach; you should find that your score has changed already, as making that choice will reduce the power of that old belief.

Coach – first question

Step back into the Coach and ask, 'What do you want?'

Present – re-score

Step back into the Present and answer what it is you want your new belief to be. In this example it might be: 'I deserve to be nice to myself like a tree stretching its branches to the sunlight.'

Coach – second question

Step back into the Coach position, and ask the second question: 'And how are you going to do that?'

In previous examples, we looked at wanting to be calm and taking yourself back to a time of being calm. In this case you will want to go:

- To a time when you did believe that you deserved to be nice to yourself.

- Or to a time when you changed a belief about something.

- Or to a time in the future when you already believe this.

As there are a number of possible memories to go to, and you might need more than one, just connect with them one at a time.

Now score the new belief, 'I deserve to be nice to myself', out of 10, where 10 is 'I totally agree' and zero is 'I don't agree'.

Brain Rehearsal

Now finish by using the Brain Rehearsal step (*see page 207*), and start to move into your life with a new, more fulfilling belief.

The next chapter presents some great tips for putting the steps into practice and overcoming any other blocks to getting a life you love, NOW.

CHAPTER 4
Lesson 21: Tips and FAQs

This chapter is a collection of some of the most important tips I've learned from people using these steps to change their lives. It also answers some of the most commonly asked questions, and considers how to use the steps to get the best results as quickly as possible.

IF THEY CAN DO IT, THEN SO CAN I – SUPERCOACHES
Throughout the history of this process thousands of people have used these steps to get exactly the kind of change that you wish for, dramatically increasing their levels of happiness, fulfilment and success.

It can be inspiring to remember that others have already travelled along this exact same path, and if they achieved the goals you wish for, using these tools, then you can too.

You can even add them to a group of Supercoaches who are there to help your Coach be the best Coach they can be. Very often people like to visualize me, or other exceptional Coaches they've experienced, as part of this supportive team, who are there encouraging you and your Coach onwards.

STYLE
I've found that paying attention to how you perform the process as a whole can be very important. Once again, the style you choose should be the opposite of the Pit you've just noticed.

For example, if it's a Pit of stress, then start to move between the process steps, and perform each step in the opposite style (i.e. very calmly). Move calmly to the Stop position and then say the Stop calmly, moving gracefully and calmly from each position to the next. Coach slowly and calmly. Keep your voice calm and measured. Doing this activates so much more of the neurology of calmness than you would if you just did it quickly.

Equally, if the Pit is 'feeling flat and tired' then do the steps of the process energetically, with enthusiasm and precision, ensuring your voice and movements are congruent with that energetic feeling.

IS IT EVER OKAY TO TALK ABOUT MY PROBLEMS?

Yes it is. There are times when it is very life-enhancing to say what's going on for you and just let it out. However, be wary of spending too much time just venting endlessly about problems. Unless there is a move towards resolving the issue it soon starts to be come un-life-enhancing and at that point moves you towards the Pit. Again this is a subtle distinction; and when to move on is your call and depends on the circumstances.

WHICH ISSUE TO WORK ON?

Often people will report they start working on one issue that takes them into the Pit and while they are resolving it another issue comes up. What should they do?

I would always recommend stopping working on the current issue and refocusing on the new interrupting one. The reason for this is that if you were to continue working on the first issue you would be doing so while being in the Pit. It's therefore quite unlikely you'll be able to be congruent as a Coach, or answer the Coaching questions effectively while distracted by being in the Pit.

MAKING THE 'TAKE MYSELF BACK MEMORY' REALLY POWERFUL

We covered this in some detail earlier (*see page 188*); however, it's worth remembering what makes for a compelling memory.

- Choose a good-quality memory and make sure you're fully IN it, recalling it in detail and using the present tense, as though it's happening now.

- Make sure the memory is not polluted by some negative event that surrounds it, and that you're not remembering it as 'it upsets me that I can't do this any more'.

If you can't get into a good powerful state using this step of the process it will probably be for one of two reasons. Either you don't believe you can access powerful positive states (in which case you need to visit the previous chapter on beliefs, *see page 219*, to resolve this) or you're not using one of the components above, which are vital for building powerful feelings from a memory.

Above all, remember if you can get into negative states then you are very good at getting into states; you just need to practise getting to the states that you wish to be in even more.

If, while accessing a good-quality memory, you find yourself just drifting (dûing drifting) out of that memory, it is often enough just to catch yourself and guide your mind straight back to the good-quality memory, without having to go through every single step of the process. This is an example of how you can start to shortcut the process as you become more familiar with it.

USING THE STEPS OVER TIME

Very often your Stop will change over time, as you develop a familiarity with the best way to interrupt negative patterns. You'll also find you need to use it less as your brain starts to learn new ways of thinking.

Sometimes you will need to step into the Choice for longer than other times, as described in the section on looping (*see page 243*).

GETTING **WHAT YOU WANT** REQUIRES A **COMMITMENT** TO DOING **WHATEVER IT TAKES.**

The Coach will always have the same qualities and the same intention will be behind everything they say. However, over time, and in different moments, you'll find yourself drawn to be creative in exactly the words you use to coach yourself.

My book *The 10 Questions to Ask for Success* is a great asset for developing your Coaching skills in this process. It will really help with your direction and life's mission and explains a number of the advanced Coaching elements, which can be used in conjunction with the steps of this book.

KEEP IT FRESH

If you go to a concert to see a band that you love, you want them to perform at their best. You wouldn't want them to be bored with their songs and perform in a jaded way. If they did, there would be no point buying a ticket.

In the same way, make sure that your coaching, and congruence in every single position, is the best it could be every single time.

When you ask the two Coaching questions, make sure you answer them based on what you want right now. If you just give the same answer each time (e.g. 'a great life') it will become tedious.

In the same way, make sure the states you choose to go back to are the best ones for that situation; so don't always say 'happy and relaxed' just because that's what you normally say as an answer.

CAN I SAY 'STOP' MORE THAN ONCE?

Yes, you can, if that helps. Although, generally, once is enough, if it's a powerful and congruent Stop. Moving into the next phases of the process will also trigger different and more useful pathways than just repeating the Stop. I would certainly suggest avoiding just shouting 'Stop!' at yourself endlessly, as that is just a simple interrupting and distracting pattern, while the process has the potential to be much more subtle and life-changing than that.

CHAPTER 5

Lesson 22: Choice and Overcoming Blocks

Occasionally people find they use the steps of the process but keep on ending up in the Pit; this is called 'looping'.

For example, they spot that they're heading towards the Pit and notice they are becoming/dûing unpleasant to themselves – thinking they're unworthy of nice things happening in their lives – they Stop, make a Choice and Coach themselves. The Coach says all the right things and is congruent, and they feel acknowledged when they step into the square of the Present. Everything seems fine; however, suddenly they're back in the Pit again, and with the same feelings of thinking they are unworthy of nice things happening in their lives.

The next step would be to say Stop again and repeat the process, knowing that by repetition these new pathways become established. Sometimes people find this doesn't happen and they just keep on looping round and round without making much progress. This is a good time to use the Choice position in more depth.

GETTING CLEAR ABOUT YOUR CHOICE

If you find yourself looping, use your Stop, and when you move to the Choice position pause here. From this position, look at the consequences of continuing to sell yourself this version of reality.

If you continue to convince yourself of the truth of the statement, for example, 'I am unworthy,' what will be the consequences?

The consequences are likely to be a continuation of what you've already had in life by believing this statement. Ask yourself, 'How many more years am I prepared to run this pattern – one, two, five, 10?'

Really facing up to the reality of the Choice you're making to somehow continue to buy into this belief is enough to recognize that this way of thinking has to go.

Having made that choice, authentically this time, the process can continue without any further looping. Occasionally, you may need to just remind yourself of that choice by standing in the position of Choice.

Choice and guilt

Sometimes people get stuck with old inherited rules about guilt. The position of Choice can be very useful for helping to resolve this. Let's look at an example:

Someone rings you up because they need some help cleaning their house before a dinner party. You are not their cleaner, but in the past you've helped out, even if you didn't want to, because that's what people do, and you just feel you can't say no.

Pit

Having scored one out of 10 in terms of being clear about a decision, we know we're in the Pit.

Now, it is clearly not bad to help people out, but we also need to make sure it fits with what our needs are too. We need to get to a position where we can make a clear choice, rather than a compulsion, about whether we help out this time or not.

Stop

So say 'Stop' to our knee-jerk response of just saying 'yes' for an easy life. We move to Choice.

HOW MANY **MORE** **YEARS** AM I PREPARED TO RUN THIS **PATTERN** ON **MYSELF?**

Choice

Pausing there, with the freedom to choose, we consider the consequences of going along with what they want:

- What does that cost us?
- Is that what we want?
- Does it fit with our plans?
- Is this important enough?
- Are we doing it just because that's what we always do, because we don't want to upset them, because we don't want them to think ill of us?

In this process, we start to realize whether we are making a choice out of love and kindness, which would move us towards a life we love, or making a choice out of guilt or fear, which will take us towards the Pit. We start to see that we need to choose to work out a solution not from the Pit but from the Coaching position.

Coach

We step into the Coach and use the acknowledgement step, and then begin to ask ourselves the important question, 'What do you want?'

If the answer is, 'To make a decision without guilt,' then we should spot the negative want and as the Coach ask for a clear positive version of this statement. Step into the Present to reply.

Present – re-score

We say, 'To make a decision based on whether I want to do it, and if this is important enough to make me change my current plans.' We notice our score has increased.

Coach

Answering the 'and how are you going to do this?' question becomes simple.

Present – re-score

It's a plan: 'I am going to look at this clearly based on how much time I have available and what I have planned.'

And a state: 'I'm going to do it from a place of "I deserve to be free to make this choice." I'm going to get into that state by stepping into the shoes of someone who is able to make these kinds of decisions easily, and feels good and complete about their choices.'

We now notice we are feeling very clear about what we want.

Brain Rehearsal

We use the Brain Rehearsal step to get familiar with this experience and with making good decisions, by taking ourselves 10 years into the future where we have done this so many times it's natural for us. We bring those feelings back to ourselves and pour them into the experience of ringing that friend and giving them the news of our decision on this occasion.

If, later on, we feel ourselves starting to dû guilt again about it, we use the process once again to get clear about our decision and why it is fine to make that.

Obviously, I'm not suggesting you use the process to go out of your way to be an unpleasant person and then excuse yourself for it, as there is no real congruence in that approach. Instead, use it to work out what fits in your life, as defined by you; sometimes you will want to say yes, other times the answer will be no, but both times they will be coming from a place of authentic choice.

It won't even be a case of, 'Do I like doing that? – Yes I'll do it' or 'I don't like it – so, no I won't do it', as sometimes it is life-enhancing to help someone out even if it's inconvenient and a job you don't like much, but you *choose* to do it because it fits with a life you love, based on weighing up all the factors involved.

IS GRIEF A VERSION OF THE PIT?

The simple answer is no. The reason for this is although it's a 'sad' emotion and you might think it is negative, the question to ask is,

'Is it life-enhancing?' And the answer is usually yes. It's important to be with how it feels to have lost someone close to you.

However, there comes a time when that grief is no longer needed, appropriate or useful. Only you can decide when that is.

If you lost a hamster when you were 12, and 20 years later you still cry about it daily, that might be a time to use the process to resolve it, but it's entirely your decision.

Moving On and Choice

One of the things that can keep people stuck is a sense that if they moved on it might betray the memory of someone who is no longer with them. A good example of this is a person who lost someone close to them some time ago, but now they fear if they were to have a good time and move on in their lives it would in some way be dishonouring their lost one.

Move to the Stop calmly; the purpose of the calm Stop here is to place a pause on this conversation so that we can look at it in more detail.

Moving to the Choice position we can ask 'If that person was here now, what would they want for us? Would they want us to go this way or that?'

The answer is very clear; they would want us to have a life we love. So, to honour them authentically, maybe it's time to make some new choices.

CHAPTER 6

Lesson 23: Consistency, Editing and Perfectionism

Consistency is one of the secrets to success in any field, but especially when training your brain.

You'll remember, I described neuroplasticity as being the same as training a set of muscles. If you overdevelop one set of muscles, and then wish to get a different set of muscles to be even stronger, then you just need to exercise consistently the muscles that you want to develop. It would be crazy to spend more time working the muscles that are already overdeveloped.

The horse and the forest

If you go to a riding stable to learn to ride, they will usually give you the gentlest and slowest horse, as this horse is ideal for learning on. You mount and ride around the small paddock, feeling rather pleased with yourself and your developing horsemanship.

The horse is very happy too. He doesn't have to work too hard, or carry you too far, and after a short time he's back in his stable eating hay.

This very pleasant arrangement continues for a while until you feel you want more adventure. You wish to ride through forests and take off to the mountains. But the horse doesn't really want to do that; he's become very used to his comfortable life. So on the first day that you steer the horse towards the forest and mountains, he's quite reluctant to go. He was expecting to go around the paddock and back to the stable. But you're the boss, so he follows your commands and heads towards the forest.

As you move towards the forest you gaze at the trees and the rivers and forget to steer your horse.

And guess where the horse heads off?

Yes, he turns his head slowly towards the paddock and before you know it, you're no longer heading in the direction you want to go.

As soon as you notice this, you stop the horse in its tracks and steer once more towards the forest. Once again, as you head towards the forest and you take your eye off the horse, the horse begins to drift back towards the path to the stables.

Unless you keep an eye on this horse he'll continue to follow his previous training of just going round the paddock. However, once he clearly understands that there's a new plan to always go to the forests and mountains, then he will learn to do that, too.

If one day you take him into the mountains, and the next three days you just take him round the paddock, he'll never get a clear idea of where he is supposed to go. He needs consistency.

Your brain is very much like that well-trained horse. It needs to know that the Pit used to be the old route, but there's a new plan now, living a life you love. And if you run those pathways consistently, and congruently, then that is what you will get.

EDITING

Linked to the idea of consistency and neuroplasticity is the vital concept of editing, briefly introduced in the ELF (Excellence of Limited Function) section (*see page 87*), but let's recap:

Imagine on a trip to London you took lots of photos. When you got home you sorted your photos out into piles: one pile of great photos and the other of photos that were blurred, dim or uninteresting. After sorting them, you then choose to discard one pile. This is the process of editing – selecting and focusing on just that pile.

It would be a bit odd if, once you'd sorted your photos, you spend all your time viewing, sharing with your friends or framing your blurred, dim and uninteresting ones. And yet that is what we do inside our heads so much of the time.

We have an incredible tendency to focus on the bad memories, on the times when we didn't perform well, when friends let us down or when things didn't turn out as we hoped. And we spend so little time, on the whole, focusing on the great memories. And yet we know which memories are likely to take us into the Pit and which ones are likely to take us to a life we love.

You may have noticed when you worked on creating positive words (*see page 170*), how many negatives ones you had ready to use in an instant. And when you were asked to take yourself back to a time when you were relaxed and happy it was less easy to find the pathway back to the good times than it was to remember a time of stress or upset. Nerve pathways that aren't used very much, just like pathways in the wild, quickly become overgrown and more difficult to use. We therefore need to become much more expert at editing in a positive and life-enhancing way.

What's to celebrate?

Many years ago I saw someone who felt he'd never been happy or able to be close to his partners – he'd had five wives. When I asked him 'What positive changes have you noticed?', he replied, 'None'.

His wife was with us too, and I asked her if she'd noticed anything. She was absolutely over the moon, she felt that for the first time she had a happy husband, who was able to be close and genuinely show his feelings for her. In fact, he had said he felt as contented as a Buddha all afternoon and evening and couldn't stop smiling.

When I turned back to him and asked him what he made of this, he said that his wife's comments had reminded him that this was exactly how he had felt all yesterday, and it was amazing.

Intrigued, I asked him why he'd said 'not much had changed' just a few minutes earlier, and he realized, to his astonishment, it was because that morning he'd woken up with a headache, which had become the entire focus of his answer, and so he'd simply 'edited out' yesterday's changes.

Now, that's an example of editing at a genius level. He had managed to remove all the incredible positives of such a fantastic change, with one tiny thought.

Watch out for bad editing; it is the easiest way to prevent any change from lasting, or making a real impact. Good editing, however, will create these new nerve pathways that lead you towards a life you love.

Exercise: Important daily exercise

For the next two weeks take five minutes every evening to focus on your day by asking:

* What positive changes have I noticed in the last few days?

This is an incredibly powerful question. And, as with many of the questions in this book, it needs to be answered very particularly.

Your answer must be purely positive, with no reference to any negative whatsoever.

At the end of this chapter you'll have an opportunity to mention the negatives, but in a very structured way that allows you to look at what you need to do to change them. It's essential not to talk about positives and negatives at the same time because it doesn't give you any chance to get your brain (just like that horse) moving into the new positive pathways of a great life.

Spotting bad edits

There are so many common 'wrong' answers to the question: 'What positive changes have I noticed?' because bad editing seems to be rampant in our society. For example:

Talking about what hasn't changed

For example, 'I still felt some anxiety'– this is the opposite answer to what the question and the editing process require. The solution is to stop yourself immediately and remind yourself that your purpose here is **just** to talk about positives.

Talking in negative wants

For example, 'I had less ANXIETY' – we should know by now that this is just going to wake up exactly the wrong neurology.

Lack of congruence

Any signs of incongruence show that, while you are talking and thinking about the positives, you are also dipping into the negative pathways at the same time, for example:

1. Mixed messages:

- 'It was good, but...' – undermines the positives with 'buts'. Silent buts are clear indicators that problems have also occurred, e.g. 'It was good (but...)'

- 'It started out quite positively' – tells you that although it started out *quite* (mixed good and bad) positively, it didn't last and ended up negatively.

- 'It was mainly/fairly positive' – which refers instantly to the negatives that also accompanied the positives. Think about the phrase 'Would you like a glass of water that is mainly/fairly clear of poisons?'

2. Qualifiers:

- 'The change was okay, I guess.'

- 'I think it was an improvement' – meaning although it's better, there's still a lot wrong with it, which refocuses us on the problems that are unchanged, rather than our successes.

Physical and vocal congruence: this is where the meaning of the positive sentence is undermined by the tonality or gestures of how you say it. Saying 'it was great' while sounding like you'd rather never do it ever again, or that it was as exciting as watching paint dry, destroys the positivity of the words.

Solutions

Cut these qualifying or undermining words, pauses and thoughts out of your description of positive change. Increase the quality of your positive language to use many more powerful and evocative words. Just like the 'big' words you learned to use to Coach yourself (*see page 173*), the bigger the words the more neurology is activated.

Doing this will transform those weakly positive statements to full-on positive ones: 'It was good (but...)' to 'It was fantastic!'

And don't get suckered into thinking 'but am I lying or just making it up?' This bigger, more 'up' description is still true; the positive change that you got was positive change.

Change is what's called a 'digital phenomenon' – there are only two possibilities: yes, there was change or, no, there wasn't any at all. Just like being pregnant, you either are or aren't. You can't be a bit pregnant. Change either happened or it didn't happen.

So any change should be celebrated – it doesn't matter whether it is small or large; it is still change. If you have created change it means you have made a difference. If you can make a difference in something that has been stuck for a long time then it tells you that you can influence it. And if you can change it then it's changeable and you can make even more difference with practice. It is very important to capitalize on change. This editing process, as the examples below illustrate, gives you the tools to do that.

'It started out quite positively'

Let's imagine this is referring to a day when you made a massive change in the morning, but by lunchtime you felt a bit flat. You can change this answer to focus on the positive changes, as required

ALL **CHANGE** SHOULD BE **CELEBRATED** – WHETHER IT'S **SMALL** OR **LARGE**, IT IS **STILL** A **CHANGE.**

by the question, of the morning, listing whatever they were in detail, as in this example: 'I got out of bed and felt incredibly alert, happy and ready for the day. It was fabulous to feel this way. I felt Present and positive I got so much done.'

It would be a waste of this very positive and successful morning's experience to destroy it by focusing entirely on the events at lunchtime. Not everything is going to change immediately, but if you destroy any positives by focusing on the negatives while in the process of change you just won't feel that you're making any headway, and you risk becoming despondent and giving up.

'It was mainly positive'

Deal with this by just deleting the word referring to the negatives, which also accompanied the positives, and change it to: 'It was such a positive experience.' Again this is true, it's just particularly focusing on those moments of time when you felt you were making headway.

The following answers are dealt with in a very similar way:

- 'The change was okay, I guess,' *changes to* 'The change was awesome.'

- 'I think it was an improvement' *changes to* 'It felt really different.'

If you don't feel comfortable being that positive or excitable then recognize this is something you are dûing. The question you need to ask next is, 'Is it useful for me?'

If you want to get real lasting neurological change, then the answer is 'It's not'; and you need to use the steps of the process to resolve this too. If you want to have a life you love, then I'd strongly recommend keeping this important question in the forefront of your mind: What positive changes have I noticed?

PERFECTIONISM

Perfectionism is linked to editing and can be a huge problem. Perfectionism is the attempt to do everything perfectly, and, on the surface, that doesn't seem like an unreasonable or bad thing. Certainly, we all want to do our best. But the problem with perfectionism is that it's not actually achievable, as it's not about being our best but setting an unattainable goal, that of absolute perfection.

Anyone with/dûing perfectionism will tell you that, even when they get 100 per cent in an exam, they still knew what was wrong with their answers, how they could have done even better and, as a result, the success felt hollow and unfulfilling.

This dissatisfaction can spread everywhere, as people dûing perfectionism get no sense of satisfaction with anything they do; they are brilliant at editing, but unfortunately they edit for imperfection, and nothing matches up to their exacting standards. They don't just demand these standards of other people, they demand them of everything, and especially of themselves.

The deliberate mistake

In the Middle East, there is a long history of incredibly skilled master carpet weavers who are able to create some of the finest, most beautiful geometric works of art known to man. The exquisite and intricate designs take years to create and weave. A master carpet weaver is a rare combination of true artist and skilled mathematician. However, in every single carpet they weave, they ensure they leave at least one flaw in the design, on purpose.

Why do you think they do that?

The answer is that they are raised to believe that only Allah is perfect. They acknowledge they are incredibly good at making carpets, but also want to show that they don't consider themselves to be on the same level as Allah. And so, with each small flaw, they remind themselves, and the world, of the greatness of Allah.

This is the problem with perfection. To be perfect you have to be god-like and, as humans, we are not. We can never achieve true perfection; we can only do our best, and know that we are good enough.

Dedicating yourself to trying to achieve perfection may be something you have done for a long time. Now you need to Stop, then stand in the position of Choice for a while and consider:

- Does this work for me?
- Does it produce happiness and fulfilment?
- What does it cost me?

Then, after answering these questions honestly, perhaps realize that it's time to give this up because, if you do want a life you love, I'm sorry to tell you, it is simply not compatible with being a perfectionist.

This doesn't mean you let go of being your best, doing what you can and want to do; it doesn't mean living in dirty squalor, or being someone who doesn't keep their word. It's not that kind of 'either or' situation. It just means letting go of the impossible slave driver that is perfection; and starting to be kind, compassionate and acknowledging yourself.

So make your choice now – a life you love or frustrated perfectionist, which would you love to have?

THINGS THAT HAVE YET TO CHANGE

Although it is so vital to focus on the positives, identifying what hasn't changed yet is also important, as it will help us become aware of what else we need to apply this book to. Naturally we need to do this is a way that just recognizes the issues without immersing ourselves in them, as that would just take us back to the Pit. If you find yourself doing that, catch yourself and instead simply take any unresolved issues as just 'feedback' and apply the process to them one at a time, until you get the change you wish for – and as you've now got these skills and you're a genius after all, that will be easier than you ever imagined.

CONCLUSION

The End

Although this chapter is titled 'The End' it is, of course, just the beginning of your real adventure.

This book can only be a guide, and having a guidebook and just reading it instead of visiting the new land is not really the point of it, it needs to be used in the field.

Before you go, there are a few final ideas to share and checks to perform to make sure you've everything you need for your trip, then I'll wave goodbye as you set out to fully explore the new world on your map.

KEEP IN TOUCH

You've learned some amazing ways of thinking and speaking, but probably realized that they are not very common in the world at the moment. So how do you keep this way of thinking alive, when most people don't generally support it yet?

Others have found linking with me and the other people who've used these skills to move their lives on is invaluable. The easiest way to do this is to visit www.lifeyoulovenow.com where you'll also find a wealth of support materials and specific seminars, to help you put these skills into practice (*see page 301–302*). I'd also really love to hear what positive changes you've made by using these skills.

There's also the *Get the Live You Love NOW* TV show, which is currently available free on iTunes, along with my other podcasts –

just search for my name. You'll find them really useful in keeping these skills alive and fresh.

FINAL CHECKS

Just like packing everything you need into your explorer's trunk before you head off, here's a final check of what you've now got onboard. By reading this book and putting it into practice have you recognized:

- How much you've already changed? Yes/No
- How much you filter for 'bad'? Yes/No
- What signs alert you to getting into the Pit? Yes/No
- What passive language patterns are? Yes/No
- Your limiting beliefs? Yes/No
- And do you now know that you can resolve your issues, achieve your goals and get a Life You Love NOW? Yes/No

This final question is, of course, one of the most important in the book. If you can agree that it's possible to get a life you love, and you now feel you're able to do that, then your future has a new positive certainty to it. You have become the most influential force for good, happiness and fulfilment in your life, which is great news because that is your main role in life.

THE WHOLE PICTURE

And speaking of roles, it's worth discussing something not mentioned before. During the process, we've separated out a number of elements essential for change and inhabited them one at a time: you've taken the role of an interrupter in the Stop position; been the wise chooser in the Choice position; been supportive, insightful and inspirational in the Coach position; and 'yourself' coming up with the answers in the Present.

But, of course, you've actually been 'you' in all the positions; these roles are all completely you. You've just focused on specific attributes of yourself, in particular moments, by stepping into those positions.

Ultimately, you've separated these elements, built them up individually, so that you can once again reintegrate all these aspects of yourself into one complete, brilliant whole. A 'you', which as you start to work out what you truly want in each moment, becomes a more fully expressed and complete version of who you really are.

Recognizing this, we see that, although the process could be seen as a simple interrupting and blocking Pit thoughts approach, or just 'positive thinking', it's so much more than that. It is a 'holistic' exploration of who we truly and deeply are – and words such as 'holistic' and 'health' have their roots in the Greek and Proto-Germanic languages, meaning 'whole' or 'entire'. By being more ourselves and less fragmented, we increase our wholeness, our health and, through that, our happiness.

There's so much that becomes possible by using these important tools. I see it every day, in the messages people send me about how they've completely changed their lives with this simple, powerful approach to life. I hope you'll seize these ideas with vigour and see how brightly you can burn your candle and shine your light through your life, and the lives of others, as a result.

And that is, I think, one of the ultimate purposes of life. Having a great life is really important but being able to be help others to see something that awakens them to what's possible, making that kind of a contribution, brings another level of brilliance to everyone's life.

Shine bright on your journey onwards.

SEE HOW **BRIGHTLY**
YOU CAN BURN YOUR
CANDLE AND **SHINE**
YOUR **LIGHT** THROUGH
YOUR **LIFE.**

APPENDIX I

ELF: How to be Even Better at Unhappiness

Note: If you've skipped straight to this chapter it's going to get a bit weird and confusing in here for you; for it to make sense I'd strongly recommend reading the book in order instead.

WHAT IS UNHAPPINESS?

For the purpose of this book I'd include the following terms under the grey umbrella of unhappiness:

- Lack of contentment
- Lack of fun
- Lack of positivity about your future
- Feeling sadness, bleak, flat, blue, bored, jaded, down

You've probably already recognized that the ideas in this book could be used to resolve more serious issues of unhappiness, such as depression. However, this is not the purpose of this book and if you have more complex issues then it's best to work through them with an experienced practitioner trained in the Lightning Process (*for more information about finding a practitioner, see page 302*).

RECIPE FOR UNHAPPINESS

Having explored the recipe for the Low Self-esteem ELF (*see page*

84), you'll be more familiar with the slightly strange phrase:

'In order successfully to dû unhappiness you must dû the following things. It simply will not work properly if you don't.'

Let's look through the recipe book that celebrates the genius of the Unhappiness ELF (Excellence of Limited Function), but mainly at how easy it's going to be to finally fail at being a genius at it.

Step 1: Filter

You'll remember the 'filter for red' exercise (*see page 61*) where looking for red objects made red things show up?

Well, in the recipe for unhappiness, the first step is to be brilliant at filtering for:

1. More evidence of:

    » How unlucky we are.

    » How we are always let down, misunderstood and unappreciated.

    » The number of sad things, disappointments, failures and disasters that happen to us.

    » The unfairness and hopelessness of our situation.

    » The absence of good and nice things.

2. The anticipation of bad things happening.

Exception filter

To avoid 'the danger of happiness' breaking out, when nice things happen the Unhappiness ELF:

*   Convinces us that as it is certain that more bad things, disappointments or failures are just around the corner, this sense that 'everything is going to turn out okay' is simply a temporary illusion.

*   Deludes us into believing 'everything is improving' will only mean that, when the inevitable crushing reality of how bad everything is finally dawns on us, the immense

disappointment will make everything seem even worse.

As a result, this news that 'things seem to be going right' doesn't stand a chance – it doesn't make us feel comforted or reassured at all. Here's the filter in a handy table for quick reference:

Pattern	Single event	Creates prediction	Filter
Unhappiness	One thing goes wrong in the morning	The whole day is ruined	Signs that everything is going wrong; things to be disappointed about

So you can see that if you are good at running the Unhappiness ELF then:

- If something goes wrong, you start to dû unhappiness;
- And if something goes right, you also instantly start to prepare for the unhappiness that you know is coming.

When you see it this way you can see how perfectly designed it is as a foolproof mechanism for getting you to stay unhappy. Truly a work of genius!

Exercise: ELF Check

Do you sometimes use any of the above filters?

Yes/No

When you dû that does it get you a life you love?

Yes/No

Remember, these are things you dû, so there will be some times when you aren't dûing them; naturally, in those times, you won't experience unhappiness.

The Power and fragility of the ELF

It is easy to see how this will rapidly cause a spiral of unhappiness, yet in spite of its powerful appearance this ELF is also fundamentally a fragile and easily exposed confidence trick.

Failing at the ELF

Notice what happens when we consider what would naturally result from swapping these filters, and instead:

1. We looked for more evidence of:

   » How lucky, supported, understood and appreciated we are

   » The abundance of great things, successes, achievements and positive events that have happened already, or are just around the corner

   » How we can recognize that we are being rewarded for what we do

   » Why we should have a sense of certainty and hopefulness about the future.

2. We anticipated the world would be accepting of us.

3. We had the opposite 'exception filter'. If ever things seemed to be 'going a bit wrong' we knew this was going to be a temporary situation. We know there's no point in fooling ourselves into believing it's going to stay that way, it's not as important as it seems and change is just around the corner.

Clearly, taking this on, a sort of 'learned optimism', as Marty Seligman[11], the father of positive psychology would say, produces a very different, and much more fulfilling version of the world.

If, when reading this, it strikes you as a distorted way of looking at reality, you would in some ways be right. However, it's no less distorted than the Unhappiness ELF, which is a distortion that discards any positivity and amplifies all negativity to exactly the same extent. If this ELF can be so powerfully disruptive in our lives, then starting to put energy into excellence of happiness will have an equal, yet opposite, effect. The question to ask is probably not 'is this a distortion?' but:

Which one would you rather have?

Step 2: Edit, distort and connect in problematical situations

This, in common with the other ELF recipes, uses the familiar words of generalizations:

- Every time
- All
- Never
- Always

- Each time
- As usual
- Forever
- Nobody/no one, etc.

But, due to the specific focus of the Unhappiness ELF, the types of phrases used are different from other ELFs.

Unhappiness generalizations
- '**Every single** time I think things are getting better, something bad **always** happens.'
- 'Now the **whole** day is ruined.'
- 'Nothing good **ever** lasts.'

Exercise: ELF check

Do you sometimes find yourself using these ways of thinking or speaking?

Yes/No

When you dû that does it get you a life you love?

Yes/No

Failing at the ELF
Notice what happens when you use that simple question mark approach: '**Every single** time I think things are getting better, something bad **always** happens.'

Ask: 'Really, "every" single time?'

Once again, this shows up how fragile the ELF is and how easy it is to disrupt it.

Step 3: Step into nasty; step away from nice
As mentioned earlier (*see page 90*):

- Stepping into a feeling and reliving it increases it – steps it up.

- Being out of it and observing it decreases it – fades it out.

Pattern	Step into	Step away from
Unhappiness	Unhappy, bad feelings and painful experience	Pleasure, good times and good feelings

To maintain high levels of unhappiness, ensure that whenever possible you step fully into Unhappiness and bad feelings, and immerse yourself in painful experiences. Disregarding positive experiences, not stepping into or enjoying pleasurable and fun feelings will also massively help in maintaining unhappiness.

Exercise: ELF check

Do you sometimes find yourself devaluing or distancing yourself from positive memories and experiences, and immersing yourself in disempowering or negative memories or anticipations?

Yes/No

When you dû that does it get you a life you love?

Yes/No

ELF: How to be Even Better at Unhappiness

Failing at the ELF
It's easy to see that if we just switch this around, so we immerse ourselves in positive life-affirming memories, anticipations or experiences and step away from the disempowering ones, then the whole ELF just falls apart, and instead we become a genius at happiness.

Step 4: Relationship to time
We can see from the chart below the specific uses of time in the Unhappiness ELF:

Pattern	Past	Present	Future
Unhappiness	Bad, should have been different	Polluted by past	More of the same

To develop a strong experience of unhappiness, it really helps to focus fully on how bad you're feeling now, to the exclusion of anything else good in your life, ever. It's also important to focus on what has happened and how bad it was, or how you should have done it differently. Finally, trust implicitly that this poor state of affairs will continue, forever.

Exercise: ELF check

Do you sometimes find yourself having these kinds of relationships to your past, present and future?

Yes/No

When you dû that does it get you a life you love?

Yes/No

269

Failing at the ELF

It's easy to see that if we just change any part of this, then the whole ELF just falls apart, and instead when we take on a 'happiness approach' to time, we become a genius at happiness.

Step 5: Internal negative soundtrack

Good indicators of playing an internal negative soundtrack include phrases such as:

- 'Oh heck' (or possibly something stronger)
- 'Not again!'
- 'Why?'
- 'It's not fair.'

It also really helps if you can include any phrases that discount or marginalize any periods of happiness and contentment, especially those that compare your life negatively to others or predict a bleak future.

Exercise: ELF check

Do you have a negative soundtrack that sometimes encourages unhappiness?

Yes/No

When you dû that does it get you a life you love?

Yes/No

Failing at the ELF

If this is your ELF, you should recognize some of these examples. Imagine if you started to say the opposite things to yourself with the same conviction and authority that you currently use to tell yourself the negative things – just notice what would naturally happen, as a result. If you start to *do* (consciously and intentionally) the things that people with happiness dû without thinking, then the ELF couldn't work any more and you'd naturally start to feel the same about yourself as they do about themselves.

Step 6: Physiology

To maintain unhappiness it really helps to increase inertia, reduce physical activity and sigh more. Research shows that exercise is a good antidote for depression.[12] Therefore, any avoidance of exercise or movement always helps to maintain the Unhappiness ELF.

Exercise: ELF check

Do you sometimes notice your posture encourages feelings of unhappiness in certain situations?

Yes/No

When you dû that does it get you a life you love?

Yes/No

Failing at the ELF

Simply moving yourself around differently, being more active or changing your posture will prevent effective running of this ELF.

Step 7: Lacking a sense of control

When any one of the ELFs is at work, it really feels as if it's all just happening to us and there is very little we can do about it. It's as if we just have to wait for it to pass, which puts us completely in the passive, powerless position of a victim – discussed in the chapter on Dû (*see page 51*).

It also leaves us with the sense that, since we can't sort it, we're therefore reliant on others to fix it. We feel we must need someone else's support or an external remedy, such as friends, drugs or therapy to cure or stop it. This is a problem, especially when we find those external supports either don't work or simply aren't always available when we need them – what do we do then?

With unhappiness, the fact that we can't even sort out our own lives makes us completely doubt our ability to be happy and creates one of the many beautifully designed destructive, self-perpetuating spirals that populate so many areas of life and create trouble for us.

Failing at the ELF

As soon as we begin to recognize we do have some power, this piece of the ELF 'machinery' melts away. This is because the ELF thrives on, and needs you to have, a sense of powerlessness to keep you trapped in it; once you've seized back the reins of control, the ELF just can't function and it completely fails.

Having looked through this pattern, you should have noticed that when you dû unhappiness you use these styles of thinking. And when you don't think in that way, you don't feel 'unhappy'.

Consider the bit of the recipe that you use most often – check out what would happen if, instead of dûing what you normally do, you started to do the opposite – what would happen to those feelings of unhappiness then?

APPENDIX II

ELF: How to be Even Better at Stress

Note: If you've skipped straight to this chapter it's going to get a bit weird and confusing in here for you; for it to make sense I'd strongly recommend reading the book in order instead.

WHAT IS STRESS?

For the purpose of this book I'd include the following terms within the frantic carnival of stress:

- Lack of peace, overthinking, worrying, catastrophizing.
- Lack of calm.
- Concern about your future.
- Feeling tense, pressured, nervous and jittery.

You've probably already recognized that the ideas in this book could be used to resolve more serious anxiety disorders. However, this is not the purpose of this book and if you have more complex issues then it's best to work through them with an experienced practitioner trained in the Lightning Process (*for more information about finding a practitioner see page 302*).

RECIPE FOR STRESS

Having explored the recipe for the Low Self-esteem ELF (*see page 84*), you'll be more familiar with the slightly strange phrase:

'In order successfully to dû stress you must dû the following things. It simply will not work properly if you don't.'

Let's look through the recipe book that celebrates the genius of the Stress ELF, and how easy it's going to be to finally fail at being a genius at it.

Step 1: Filter

You'll remember filters from the 'filter for red' exercise (*see page 61*) where looking for red things made red things show up. Well, in the recipe for stress, the first step is to be brilliant at filtering for:

1. More evidence of:

   » How dangerous or scary everything is (although we may logically know they are unrealistic evaluations).

   » What is about to go wrong or what is already going wrong.

   » Why we should be worried and what we should worry about.

2. The anticipation of scary/worrying things happening.

Exception filter

To avoid the danger of calmness breaking out, when things seem to be going to plan and no disasters have occurred the Stress ELF:

- Convinces us that as it is certain there's a catastrophe or disaster coming, this sense of 'everything turning out okay' is simply a temporary illusion. This is actually the classic 'calm before the storm' feeling.

- Deludes us into believing 'everything is fine' is foolish. Doing that will only mean that we will let our guard down so badly that when the inevitable crisis strikes we will be unprepared, vulnerable and completely unable to cope.

As a result, when everything is going to plan it's therefore very worrying and unsettling and a sure sign a very forceful storm is about to hit us, probably from an unexpected direction – we should in fact increase our alertness.

Here's the filter in a handy table for quick reference:

Pattern	Single event	Creates prediction	Filter
Stress	We make plans	Plans always go wrong	What could go/is going to go wrong?
Stress	One thing goes to plan	Oh no! This false sense of calmness is just setting me up for a bigger fall when things start to go wrong, as they are just about to	Even calm periods are just the signal that a fearful period is beginning; all moments are seen as the same (dangerous)

So you can see that if you are good at running the Stress ELF then:

- If something goes wrong, you start to get stressed;
- And if something goes right, you also instantly start to prepare for the stress that you know is coming.

When you see it this way you can see how perfectly designed it is as a foolproof mechanism for getting you to stay stressed; again truly a work of genius!

Exercise: ELF check

Do you sometimes use any of the above filters?

Yes/No

When you dû that does it get you a life you love?

Yes/No

Remember, these are things you dû, so there will be some times when you aren't dûing them; naturally, in those times, you won't experience stress.

The power and fragility of the ELF

As we covered earlier in the book, we can easily see how thinking this way will rapidly cause a spiral of stress, yet in spite of its powerful appearance, the ELF is fundamentally a fragile, easily exposed confidence trick.

Failing at the ELF

Notice what happens when we consider what would naturally result from swapping these filters, and instead:

1. We looked for more evidence of:

   » How successfully things turned out

   » How the world, and other people, work out pretty well without us having to control them all the time

   » How, by being calm, we made better decisions and coped better with all situations

   » How we could trust the future and others

   » How calmness was healthy and safe

   » Why we should be relaxed about the future.

2. We anticipated the world would be accepting of us.

3. We had the opposite 'exception filter'. If ever things seemed to be 'going a bit wrong' we knew this was going to be a temporary situation. We know there's no point in fooling ourselves into believing it's going to stay that way, it's not as important as it seems and change is just around the corner.

Clearly taking on this version of the world produces a very different, and much more fulfilling life experience.

If, when reading this, it strikes you as a ridiculously distorted way of looking at reality, you would in some ways be right. However, it's no less distorted than the Stress ELF, which discards any positivity and amplifies all negativity to exactly the same extent. If this ELF can be so powerfully disruptive in our lives, then starting to put energy into excellence of calmness will have an equal yet opposite effect. The question to ask is probably not 'Is this a distortion?' but:

Which one would you rather have?

Here's an interesting question: Does stress ever help?

Some people use stress to get motivated, but dûing motivation is better than dûing stress to achieve this; some people use it for planning, but calm planning works better. It seems that in any situation – with the possible exception of being chased by a tiger where the stress response physiologically gives us a temporary extra burst of speed – stress is probably our least useful response.

Step 2: Edit, distort and connect in problematical situations

This, in common with the other ELF recipes, uses the familiar words of generalizations:

- Every time
- All
- Never
- Always

- Each time
- As usual
- Forever
- Nobody/no one etc.

But because of the specific focus of the Stress ELF the types of phrases used are different from other ELFs.

Stress generalizations

- **'Every single** time I stop worrying about **everything** that's going to go wrong, that's always when **everything** goes wrong.'
- 'I have to control **everything**.'
- 'Nothing good **ever** lasts.'

Exercise: ELF check

Do you sometimes find yourself using these ways of thinking or speaking?

Yes/No

When you dû that does it get you a life you love?

Yes/No

Failing at the ELF

Notice what happens when you use that simple question mark approach: '**Every single** time I stop worrying about **everything** that's going to go wrong, that's always when **everything** goes wrong.'

'Every single time?'

Once again, the ELF shows up how fragile and how easily disrupted it can be.

Step 3: Step into nasty; step away from nice

As mentioned earlier (*see page 90*):

• Stepping into a feeling and reliving it increases it – steps it up.

• Being out of it and observing it decreases it – fades it out.

Pattern	Step into	Step away from
Stress	Anxious, stressful feelings and disastrous memories or anticipations	Calm, things working out, content and safe feelings

To maintain high levels of stress, ensure that whenever possible you step fully into anxious, stressful and disastrous memories or anticipations of events. Disregarding calm experiences, not stepping into or enjoying relaxation and the times when things worked out well will also massively help in maintaining stress.

Exercise: ELF check

Do you sometimes find yourself devaluing or distancing yourself from positive memories and experiences, and immersing yourself in disempowering or negative memories or anticipations?

Yes/No

When you dû that does it get you a life you love?

Yes/No

Failing at the ELF

It's easy to see that if we just switch this around – so we immerse ourselves in positive life-affirming memories, anticipations or experiences and step away from the disempowering ones – then the whole ELF just falls apart, and instead we become a genius at being calm, Present and happy.

Step 4: Relationship to time

We can see in the following chart the specific uses of time in the Stress ELF:

Pattern	Past	Present	Future
Stress	Stressful, should have been managed better to avoid the problems	Polluted by forthcoming crises, which have to be planned for, to avoid them as possible	Full of a million disasters – so even my detailed planning will not be sufficient to avoid them all

To develop a powerful experience of stress it really helps to focus fully on the frightening, chaotic future that's inevitably hurtling towards you. The only thing you can count on about your future is it's going to be tense and difficult and no matter how far ahead those problems may be, it's vital to feel the fear about them now.

Exercise: ELF check

Do you sometimes find yourself having these kinds of relationships to your past, present and future?

Yes/No

When you dû that does it get you a life you love?

Yes/No

Failing at the ELF

It's easy to see that if we just change any of this, then the whole ELF just falls apart, and instead when we take on a calm approach to time, we become a genius at calm.

Step 5: Internal negative soundtrack

Good indicators of playing an internal negative soundtrack include phrases such as:

- 'What if… [*for example, the disaster happens*]?'
- 'But how will I cope when… [*e.g. the disaster happens*]?'
- 'I must control… [*for example, everything*].'
- 'It's all going to go wrong.'
- 'I can't cope with this.'
- 'It's all too much.'
- 'Oh heck!' (Or, possibly, something stronger.)
- 'Not again.'
- 'Why?'
- 'It's not fair.'

It also really helps if you can also include any phrases that ensure you focus entirely on the forthcoming stressful future.

Exercise: ELF check

Do you have a negative soundtrack that sometimes encourages stress?

Yes/No

When you dû that does it get you a life you love?

Yes/No

Failing at the ELF
If this is your ELF, you should recognize some of these examples. Imagine if you started to say the opposite things to yourself with the same conviction and authority as you currently use when telling yourself the negative things – just notice what would naturally happen as a result. If you start to *do* (consciously and intentionally) the things that people with profound calmness and trust in the world dû without thinking, then the ELF couldn't work any more and you'd naturally start to feel the same about yourself as they do about themselves.

Step 6: Physiology
To maintain stress it really helps to be in overdrive, very busy, always on the go, and to hyperventilate and be very aware of all body symptoms. So any avoidance of relaxation, calmness or graceful gentle movement always helps to maintain the Stress ELF.

Exercise: ELF check

Do you sometimes notice your posture encourages feelings of stress in certain situations?

Yes/No

When you dû that does it get you a life you love?

Yes/No

Failing at the ELF

Simply moving yourself around differently, being less frenetic and changing your posture will prevent effective running of the Stress ELF.

Step 7: Lacking a sense of control

When any one of the ELFs is at work, it really feels as if it's all just happening to us and that there is very little we can do about it. It's as though we just have to wait for it to pass, which puts us completely in the passive, powerless, victim position that we discussed in the section on Dû.

It also leaves us with the sense that since we can't sort it, we're therefore reliant on others to fix it. We feel we must need someone else's support or an external remedy, such as friends, drugs or therapy to cure or stop it. This is a problem, especially when we find those external supports either don't work or simply aren't always available when we need them - what do we do then?

With stress the fact that we can't even sort our own lives out very successfully makes us completely doubt our ability to ever be calm or happy, which creates one of the many beautifully designed destructive, self-perpetuating spirals that seem to populate so many areas of life where we get into trouble.

Failing at the ELF

As soon as we begin to recognize we do have some power, this piece of the ELF 'machinery' melts away. This is because the Stress ELF thrives on, and needs you to have, a sense of powerlessness to keep you trapped in it; once you've seized back the reins of control, the ELF just can't function and it completely fails.

Having looked through this pattern, you should have noticed that when you dû stress you use these styles of thinking. And when you don't think in that way, you don't get 'stressed'.

Consider the bit of the recipe that you use most often – check out what would happen if instead of dûing what you normally do, you started to do the opposite – what would happen to those feelings of stress then?

APPENDIX III

ELF: How to be Even Better at Guilt

Note: If you've skipped straight to this chapter it's going to get a bit weird and confusing in here for you; I'd strongly recommend reading the book in order instead.

WHAT IS GUILT?

For the purpose of this book, I'd include the following terms within the embarrassment of riches that is guilt:

- Shame, self-blame and feeling foolish.

- Thinking we are selfish and thoughtless while actually being overly concerned for the happiness of others and their opinions.

The Guilt ELF (Excellence of Limited Function) triggers when we think we may have done something that is considered either by us, or by others, to be 'wrong'. If you're a familiar user of the Guilt ELF, you'll probably recall that we already covered in an earlier chapter how guilt has virtually no useful purpose whatsoever.

The Guilt ELF is also purely a result of our cultural training – one culture will consider a particular behaviour to be part of polite etiquette and another will find it totally unacceptable. The okay hand gesture used in many Western countries is a good example. Yet the gesture means 'money' in Japan, 'zero' or 'worthless' in

France, 'homosexual' in Venezuela and Turkey, and 'go away' in Brazil. If you made this gesture unwittingly in these countries you might notice a strange response from the locals – at the time you might be puzzled but not guilty. You could only feel guilty about it later, if someone told you you'd made an unintentional error. This highlights the fact that guilt is an optional learned response rather than a 'something' you inherently have.

Keep that in mind as you read on...

RECIPE FOR GUILT

Having explored the previous ELF recipes, you'll be more familiar with the slightly strange phrase:

'In order successfully to dû guilt you must dû the following things. It simply will not work properly if you don't.'

Let's look through the recipe book that celebrates the genius of the Guilt ELF and, while we're doing that, explore how easy it's going to be to finally fail at being a genius at it.

Step 1: Filter

You'll remember filters from the 'filter for red' exercise (*see page 61*), where looking for red things made red things show up. Well, in the recipe for guilt, the first step is to be really brilliant at filtering for:

1. More evidence for 'even if we didn't intend to':

    » How wrong, bad, hurtful or selfish we are.

    » Our mistakes.

    » How we always get it wrong.

    » How we are the cause of others' pain and suffering.

    » How we do nasty things.

    » How we make things turn out bad, how we spoil and ruin things.

    » Why we should feel guilty.

    » How we're thoughtless.

» How we've contravened some code or broken some rule.

» How we've let people down.

» How we don't deserve or are not worthy of something.

» How we're to blame.

» How we ought to have done something that we either are not doing or haven't done.

» How we are less good than others ('better people').

You may notice some similarity with some of the above and some of the elements of the Low Self-esteem ELF filter (*see page 84*). As a result, these two often go hand in hand; and sure enough many people with low self-esteem feel very guilty and vice versa.

2. We can also generate guilt in advance by anticipating that we might wrong someone, or feel guilty about something, well ahead of the event.

Exception filter
This ELF could be easily derailed if you:

• Feel good about yourself and what you've done.

• Clearly distinguish your responsibility for yourself from the responsibly for making everyone else okay.

So, if there are any warning signs of this breaking out, the Guilt ELF:

• Convinces us that it will all soon be wrecked by something we, unintentionally, do – or are probably doing right now without even realizing, that upsets or might upset someone else. So this sense of 'everything going to turn out okay' is simply a temporary illusion.

• Deludes us into believing 'everything is fine' will only mean that we let ourselves down even further by continuing to rush headlong into the disaster currently unfolding. This will make us feel so stupid that we didn't even see it coming.

Everything seeming to be fine is therefore very worrying, as we know we're bound to have done something wrong, and either we're not aware of it or don't even feel remorseful about it. This makes us feel guilty for not feeling guilty.

Here's the filter in a handy table for quick reference:

Pattern	Single event	Creates prediction	Filter
Guilt	We start to mess up and make things 'bad'	Just as I thought, I've made it bad for everyone	How am I ruining this? How am I embarrassing others or myself?
Guilt	I've not made anyone upset or embarrassed myself	At least, not yet! This false sense of 'okayness' is just setting me up for a bigger fall when I start to make things go wrong, as I am just about to do I am doing something 'bad'; I'm just so inept I've not even noticed it yet	Even 'okay' guilt-free periods are just a signal that I've probably already messed up or am about to; all moments are seen as the same (guilt-filled)

So you can see that if you are good at running the Guilt ELF then:

- Guilt: If something goes wrong, you start to feel guilty.

- No guilt: And if something seems to go right, you also instantly start to prepare for the guilt that is coming, or know that you've just not yet noticed what it is that you've done 'wrong'.

When you see it this way you can see how perfectly designed it is as a foolproof mechanism for getting you to stay guilty; again truly a work of genius!

Exercise: ELF check

Do you sometimes use any of the above filters?

Yes/No

When you dû that does it get you a life you love?

Yes/No

Remember, these are things you dû, so there will be some times when you aren't dûing them; naturally, in those times, you won't experience guilt.

The power and fragility of the ELF

As covered in the earlier chapters, we can easily see how this will rapidly cause a spiral of guilt, yet in spite of its powerful appearance, the ELF is fundamentally a fragile, easily exposed confidence trick.

Failing at the ELF

Notice what happens when we consider what would naturally result from swapping these filters, and instead:

1. We looked for more evidence of:
   » How successfully things turned out.
   » How we aren't responsible for the happiness of the world and for other people.
   » Knowing deep inside that it's okay not to get things right all the time.
   » How many mistakes aren't that serious in the greater scheme of things.
   » How no one gets it right all the time.
   » How people aren't that concerned or aware of most errors.
2. We anticipated the world would be accepting of us.

3. We had the opposite 'exception filter'. If ever things seemed to be 'going a bit wrong' we knew this was going to be a temporary situation. We know there's no point in fooling ourselves into believing it's going to stay that way, it's not as important as it seems and change is just around the corner.

Clearly taking on this version of the world produces a very different, and much more fulfilling life experience.

If, when reading this, it strikes you as a ridiculously distorted way of looking at reality, you would in some ways be right. However, it's no less distorted than the Guilt ELF, which discards any positivity and amplifies all negativity to exactly the same extent. If this ELF can be so powerfully disruptive in our lives, then starting to put energy into excellence of being at peace will have an equal yet opposite effect. The question to ask is probably not 'is this a distortion?' but:

Which one would you rather have?

Step 2: Edit, distort and connect in problematic situations

This, in common with the other ELF recipes, uses the familiar words of generalizations:

- Every time
- All
- Never
- Always

- Each time
- As usual
- Forever
- Nobody/no one etc.

Due to the specific focus of the Guilt ELF the types of phrases used are different from other ELFs.

Guilt generalizations
'**Every single** time I stop being guilty about **everything**, that's always when **everything** goes wrong.'
'I have to control **everything**.'
'I have to be responsible for **everyone's** feelings.'

Exercise: ELF check

Do you sometimes find yourself using these ways of thinking or speaking?
Yes/No

When you dû that does it get you a life you love?
Yes/No

Failing at the ELF

Notice what happens when you use that simple question mark approach: 'I have to be responsible for **everyone's** feelings.'

'Everyone's?'

Once again, the ELF shows up how fragile and how easily disrupted it can be.

Step 3: Step into nasty; step away from nice

As mentioned earlier (*see page 90*):

- Stepping into a feeling and reliving it increases it – steps it up.

- Being out of it and observing it decreases it – fades it out.

Pattern	Step into	Step away from
Guilt	'Wrongness', others' potential, imagined or real upset, guilt-filled feelings and memories or anticipations	Being at peace, things working out and recognizing others have a responsibility for themselves

To maintain high levels of guilt ensure that whenever possible you step fully into the guilt-filled feelings and memories or anticipations of events. Disregarding peaceful experiences, not stepping into or enjoying relaxation and the times when things worked out well, or seeing others responsibility for their own lives will also massively help in maintaining the Guilt Elf.

Exercise: ELF check

Do you sometimes find yourself devaluing or distancing yourself from positive memories and experiences and immersing yourself in disempowering or negative memories or anticipations?

Yes/No

When you dû that does it get you a life you love?

Yes/No

Failing at the ELF

It's easy to see that if we just switch this around, we immerse ourselves in positive life-affirming memories, anticipations or experiences and step away from the disempowering ones, then the whole ELF just falls apart, and instead we become a genius at being peaceful, Present and happy.

Step 4: Relationship to time

We can see from the chart below the specific uses of time in the Guilt ELF:

Pattern	Past	Present	Future
Guilt	Guilty – I should have managed those situations better to avoid the problems	Polluted by forthcoming inevitable guilt, which I have to plan for to avoid getting it wrong as much as possible	Full of a million disasters – so, even my detailed planning won't be enough to avoid them all

To develop a powerful experience of guilt, it really helps to focus fully on the guilt-laden future you are responsible for creating. The only thing you can count on about your future is it's going to be tense and difficult and no matter how far ahead those problems may be, it's vital to feel the shame about them now.

Exercise: ELF check

Do you sometimes find yourself having these kinds of relationships to your past, present and future?

Yes/No

When you dû that does it get you a life you love?

Yes/No

Failing at the ELF

It's easy to see that if we just change any of this, then the whole ELF just falls apart, and instead, when we take on an 'at peace' approach to time, we become a genius at being peaceful, Present and happy.

Step 5: Internal negative soundtrack

Good indicators of playing internal negative soundtrack include phrases such as:

- 'What have I done...?'
- 'What will they think?'
- 'I must control (everything).'
- 'I'm making it all go wrong.'
- 'I've let them down.'
- 'I should, ought to, must.'
- 'I shouldn't, ought not to, mustn't.'
- 'I feel bad that I feel guilty all the time.'

It also really helps if you can include any phrases that ensure you focus entirely on the forthcoming guilt-filled future.

Exercise: ELF check

Do you have a negative soundtrack that sometimes encourages guilt?

Yes/No

When you dû that does it get you a life you love?

Yes/No

Failing at the ELF

If this is your ELF you should recognize some of these examples. Imagine if you started to say the opposite things to yourself with the same conviction and authority as you currently use when telling yourself the negative things – just notice what would naturally happen as a result. If you start to *do* (consciously and intentionally) the things that people with profound peace and trust in themselves, and the world, dû without thinking, then the ELF couldn't work any more and you'd naturally start to feel the same about yourself as they do about themselves.

Step 6: Physiology

To maintain the Guilt Elf it really helps to be in overdrive, very busy, always on the go and to avoid relaxation and physical calmness.

Exercise: ELF check

Do you sometimes notice your posture encourages feelings of guilt in certain situations?

Yes/No

When you dû that does it get you a life you love?

Yes/No

Failing at the ELF
Simply moving yourself around differently or changing your posture will prevent effective running of the ELF.

Step 7: Lack of a sense of control
This section is quite similar for all ELFs but, as it's so important, I'll repeat it one last time. When any one of the ELFs is at work, it really feels as if it's all just happening to us and that there is very little we can do about it. We just have to wait for it to pass, which puts us completely in the passive, powerless, victim position that we discussed in the chapter on Dû (*see page 51*).

It also leaves us with the sense that since we can't sort it, it's something out of our control that we'll just have to live with.

Failing at the ELF
As soon as we begin to recognize we do have some power, this piece of the ELF 'machinery' melts away. This is because the Guilt ELF thrives on, and needs you to have, a sense of powerlessness to keep you trapped in it; once you've seized back the reins of control, the ELF just can't function and it completely fails.

Having looked through this pattern, you should have noticed that when you dû guilt you use these styles of thinking. And when you don't think in that way, you don't feel 'guilty'.

Consider the bit of the recipe that you use most often – check out what would happen if instead of dûing what you normally do, you started to do the opposite – what would happen to those feelings of guilt then?

APPENDIX IV

Handy Reference of the Steps

1. Present	
2. Spot the Pit	Quickly score yourself out of 10, where 10 is feeling good and zero is not feeling good.
3. Stop	Choose the appropriate one.
4. Choice	Ask, 'That way or this way?'
5. Coach	Acknowledge – check we have taken it in and re-score Ask 'What do you want?' Answer and re-score. Ask 'and how are you going to get it?' Answer by either taking yourself back to a time when you felt that way and/or creating an action plan – re-score.
6. End	By recognizing you are now Present again and creating a life you love.
7. Reflection and Brain Rehearsal	Ask, 'What have I learned from this, that is really useful for my future?'

Endnotes

1. Baird, B. *et al.* 'Inspired by Distraction: Mind Wandering Facilitates Creative Incubation', *Psychol Sci.,* 2012: 23(10); 1117–22

2. Howell, W.S. *The Empathic Communicator* (Wadsworth Publishing Company, 1982; 29–33)

3. There's much argument about the misattribution of this quote – Albert Einstein being the main person quoted as its author. However, there is no reliable reference to it in his papers. The most well-documented origin is from a paper by Jenson, J. 'Step 2: A Promise of Hope', *Alcoholics Anonymous*, 1980; 10

4. Russell, J. and Carroll, J. 'On the Bipolarity of Positive and Negative Affect', *Psychological Bulletin*, 1999; 125: 3–30

5. Carney, D., Cuddy, A., Yap, A. 'Power Posing: Brief Nonverbal Displays Affect Neuroendocrine Levels and Risk Tolerance', *Psychol Sci.*, 2010; 21: 1363–8

6. Hennenlotter, A. *et al*. 'The Link Between Facial Feedback and Neural Activity Within Central Circuitries of Emotion—New Insights from Botulinum Toxin–Induced Denervation of Frown Muscles, *Cerebral Cortex*, 2008; 19(3): 537–42

7. Miller, G. A. 'The Magical Number Seven, Plus or Minus Two: Some Limits on our Capacity for Processing Information', *Psychological Review*, 1956; 63(2): 81–97

8. Richter, M. *et al*. 'Do Words Hurt? Brain Activation During Explicit and Implicit Processing of Pain Words', *Pain*, 2010; 148: 198–205

9. This test was originally devised by Professor Shane Fredrick from MIT, Massachusetts, USA

10. Siegel, B. *Love, Medicine and Miracles* (Harper Perennial, 1986); 133

11. Seligman, M. *Learned Optimism* (Vintage Books, 2006)

12. Salmon, P. 'Effects of Physical Exercise on Anxiety, Depression and Sensitivity to Stress – A Unifying Theory', *Clinical Psychology Review*, 2001; 21(1): 33–61

Glossary

Coach A specific role adopted by a person in order to assist another sort out his or her particular issues. The qualities that ensure the assistance is 'Coaching' (rather than advice or interference) are:

- Coaching is only provided when there has been a request or an agreement for Coaching.

- The Coach leaves their problems at the door.

- The Coach clearly believes in you.

- The Coach assesses the feasibility of your plans. If they believe them to be sound, they will ensure that you know that what you're aiming for is entirely possible and definitely within your ability.

- The Coach always maintains a big, clear perspective, which will often be bigger and clearer than yours. This allows them to see the end point even when you can't.

- The Coach doesn't take any bull. If you've committed to achieving something and begin to cheat on yourself, talk yourself down, or not deliver on your promises, they won't stand for it.

- The Coach rarely gives advice, but mainly asks questions that assist you in discovering the solutions.

- The Coach is supportive and caring.

- The Coach listens, but will assist you to refocus if you start to go off the point or endlessly complain.
- The Coach takes the time, because they know you're important.
- The Coach has integrity; they don't just say things, they mean them.
- The Coach ensures that you have a clear sense that they understand what is going on for you.
- The Coach thinks you're important.
- The Coach gives feedback instead of criticism, and will never say 'you're wrong' (this is an identity-level statement, which implies *you* are wrong, rather than what you did was inappropriate), although they may suggest improvements to aspects of your performance.
- The Coach is able to reflect on both their own and your performance.
- The Coach brings a sense of humour and lightness to the situation.

Coaching A relationship where one person (the client or coachee) has very specifically and clearly asked for another person's (the Coach) assistance to help sort out a particular issue. The specific qualities that the 'Coach' brings to that situation will designate it as Coaching rather than advice or interference.

ELF An ELF (Excellence of Limited Function) is the technical term for upside-down genius. It describes something that 1) we have become excellent at – to a genius level – and 2) produces brilliantly disastrous results in our lives and limits our happiness. Examples of ELF's include stress, unhappiness, low self-esteem, feeling overwhelmed, perfectionism, guilt, self-doubt and overeating. Every ELF has a very particular recipe or structure; some of these are included in the book. These recipes came from my research into working out exactly what was going on in people's minds, unconsciously, when they were messing things up so effectively.

Influence Sometimes confused with 'blame' and 'responsibility' as in 'I should have influenced that' meaning 'it's my fault' or 'I'm to blame'. But, in fact, 'influence' means being able to use your abilities to take action to change something, and being able to make a difference to the way things turn out. It also means that if you've promised to do something and you haven't delivered on that promise, then it's up to you to influence things (do something) to make it right.

Neuro-linguistic programming (NLP) A system for finding out in detail how individuals achieve excellence, using a process called modelling. The modelling process is complete when enough detail has been discovered to teach that excellence to a novice and help them to achieve excellence in that field. NLP has modelled many skills (e.g. spelling, speed-reading, sharp shooting, etc.) but is also interested in the structure that underpins many issues (e.g. depression, phobias, anxiety, allergies, etc.). Learning about how we 'do' these things well allows people who currently excel at these 'skills' (depression, phobias, stress or allergies) to learn to become less proficient, to the point where they don't have the issue any more.

Outcomes These are similar to goals that we set ourselves in life, but outcomes are distinguished by having a much greater degree of thoughtfulness and specificity about them which makes them much more likely to be attained.

State This is the same as a 'state of mind' or 'feeling'. You can either be in a useful state (e.g. a state of 'confidence' in an interview) or a non-useful state (e.g. a 'nervous' state in an interview).

Neuroplasticity This is the ability of the brain to change its structure, as a result of how it is used. The nerve pathways that are most commonly used become stronger, faster and more influential on brain function as a whole. Those that are triggered together become more connected up to each other.

Resources

I do hope you've enjoyed putting the book's skills and ideas into your life; you might also find the following really useful:

Life You Love NOW seminars
A great way to put the skills and tools in this book into practice, and get even more happiness and fulfilment, is to visit www.lifeyoulovenow. com, where you'll find the most up-to-date information on this exciting range of seminars.

Other books by Phil Parker
An Introduction to the Lightning Process®
This is both an essential first step for those intending to take a Lightning Process seminar and a resource for discovering more about how this unique training programme can make a difference to your health and wellbeing.

Dû – Unlock Your Full Potential With A Word
This intriguing and life-changing book explores Phil's invention of the new word, 'Dû', introduced in *Get the Life You Love, NOW*. Discover in even greater detail how and when to use these new ideas to start to get powerful change in your life.

The 10 Questions to Ask for Success
This book develops the 'Coaching aspects' presented in *Get the Life You Love, NOW*. It helps you to recognize that you already hold the answers within you, and how to create your own solutions to almost all of life's challenges.

CD audio programmes

Phil's CD titles are designed to help you with every aspect of your life, covering topics such as de-stressing, building confidence, stopping smoking, weight loss, pregnancy support and more. Please visit: http://www.philparker.org for a full list.

Other related programmes

Health conditions

This book is specifically for happiness and fulfilment; however, the Lightning Process, on which this book is based, helps people with chronic health issues. If you wish to work with these kinds of issues then I'd recommend my other book on this subject, *An Introduction to the Lightning Process*, and working through the LP with a Registered practitioner. We have practitioners around the world; visit www.lightningprocess.com to find one near you.

Drug addictions and substance use

A development of this programme, 'The Rediscovery Process', is specially tailored for helping those dealing with drug and alcohol abuse, which has proved very successful in resolving addiction issues, as well as addressing the underlying causes of those problems.

Business performance

P4 is Phil Parker's Peak Performance business training programme, and is tailored specifically to deliver the ideas and tools in this book to business professionals to enhance their performance and resilience, and to encourage creative problem-solving. Visit www.p4training.com for more information.

NLP courses

If you enjoyed this book and want to learn more, you might also be interested in the NLP courses we run, which offer training to enhance relationships, productivity, confidence and motivation skills, change habits and increase your ability to communicate even more effectively. Visit www.philparkertraining.com to find more about our introductory and starter courses, as well as our practitioner-level training, clinical training and advanced courses.

ABOUT THE AUTHOR

Phil Parker is an internationally renowned lecturer, therapist and innovator in the field of personal development. He has changed the lives of thousands of people by designing the ground-breaking Lightning Process® seminars. He is currently undertaking a PhD at London Met University and researching the application of the Lightning Process in helping those with addiction issues.

His core principle is that people are geniuses with amazing skills, qualities and talents, and he hopes he can help as many people as possible to find that out about themselves. You can get Phil's latest thoughts, self-help tools and videos for free from his podcast, blog, Twitter and Facebook.

To contact Phil Parker please email phil@philparker.org

www.lightningprocess.com
www.philparker.org